swordfish siciliana

Swordfish belongs to the group of fish that have recently become more appreciated for their contribution of omega-3 essential oils to the diet. Swordfish is found in both the Atlantic Ocean and the Mediterranean Sea, and forms quite a large part of the Mediterranean diet, which is said to be one of the healthiest in the world.

Yield: 4 servings

4 (8-ounce) pieces of swordfish
1 small yellow onion, diced
Olive oil, for sautéing
1 teaspoon chopped garlic
1 cup pitted kalamata olives
2 cups chopped Roma tomatoes
Salt
Freshly ground black pepper
2 ounces white wine
1/2 cup fresh basil leaves
2 tablespoons capers
1 teaspoon crushed red pepper flakes
1 tablespoon unsalted butter
Whole basil leaves, for garnish

To prepare the sauce, cook the onions in the oil in a large sauté pan on medium-low heat for 10 minutes, until the onions are soft. Add the garlic, and cook for 30 seconds. Add the olives and chopped tomatoes, smashing them in the pan with a fork. Season with salt and pepper. Simmer on low heat for 15 minutes. Add the white wine, and simmer for 10 more minutes to reduce the liquid. Add the basil, capers, crushed red pepper flakes, and butter, and cook for 1 minute more.

Brush the swordfish with olive oil, and sprinkle with salt and pepper. Grill on high heat for 5 minutes on each side until the center is no longer raw. Do not overcook. Place the sauce on the bottom of a plate, arrange the swordfish on top, and garnish with basil leaves. Serve hot or at room temperature.

poached grouper WITH saffron, roasted vegetables & meyer lemon rice

Poaching can be one of the healthiest and easiest ways to prepare your fish because you can avoid adding fat by poaching in water or broth. With seafood, the possibilities are endless for healthful eating and adding variety and great taste to everyday meals.

Yield: 4 servings

4 (8-ounce) grouper fillets
Salt
Freshly ground black pepper
8 cups water or fish stock/broth
6 Meyer lemons, juiced (or any other sweet lemon)
2 tablespoons freshly chopped sage
1 shallot, roughly chopped
Pinch of salt
2 pinches saffron, divided

1 carrot, cut diagonally, 1/4-inch thick
1 julienne-cut red bell pepper
1 julienne-cut yellow bell pepper
1 small zucchini, cut diagonally, 1/4-inch thick
8 thin spears asparagus, stems partially peeled
1/4 cup olive oil
2 cups long-grain or wild-rice blend
Fresh herb sprig, for garnish

Preheat the oven to 350°F.

Season the grouper lightly with salt and pepper. In a medium sauce pan, add the water or fish stock, lemon juice, sage, shallot, a pinch of salt, and a pinch of saffron. Bring the poaching liquid to a boil. Carefully add the fish. Reduce the heat to medium-low until the fish is cooked through, about 6 to 8 minutes. Take the fish out and set aside. Strain the poaching liquid well and reserve it for later.

Place the cut vegetables in a bowl with olive oil, the remaining pinch of saffron, salt, and pepper. Mix well and lay them on a sheet pan. Roast for 5 to 10 minutes, or until tender.

Place the rice in a small pot and add enough of the reserved poaching liquid to cover the rice by 1/2 inch. Bring to a boil and reduce to medium-low heat. Once the rice is cooked, remove from the heat and set aside.

Place the rice in the center of the plate. Arrange the roasted vegetables around the rice. Carefully place the grouper atop the rice and garnish with a drizzle of olive oil and a fresh herb sprig of your choice. Enjoy!

McCORMICK & SCHMICK'S

SEAFOOD RESTAURANT COOKBOOK

SPECIAL EDITION

RECIPES COMPILED BY **Chef William King**
PHOTOGRAPHY BY **Rick Schafer**

ARNICA publishing
Portland, Oregon

The Library of Congress has cataloged the first edition as follows:

The McCormick & Schmick's Seafood Restaurant cookbook / recipes compiled by Chef William King ; photography by Rick Schafer.
    p. cm.
 ISBN 0-9745686-5-1 (hardcover : alk. paper) 1. Cookery (Seafood) 2. McCormick & Schmick's Seafood Restaurants. I.
Title: McCormick and Schmick's Seafood Restaurant cookbook. II. King, William, 1952- III. McCormick & Schmick's Seafood Restaurants.

TX747.M34 2005
641.6'92--dc22

2005013770

Second edition ISBN: 978-0-9794771-5-7
08 07 06 05   1 2 3 4 5 6

All recipes © McCormick & Schmick's Seafood Restaurants
Photography by Rick Schafer
Cover and text design by Aimee Genter

The photographs of Bill McCormick & Doug Schmick in the Introduction used courtesy of Denyce Nichols, Something Blue Photography.

Arnica Publishing, Inc.
3880 SE Eighth Ave, Suite 110
Portland, Oregon 97202
Phone: (503) 225-9900
Fax: (503) 225-9901
www.arnicacreative.com

Arnica books are available at special discounts when purchased in bulk for premiums and sales promotions, as well as for fund-raising or educational use. Special editions or book excerption can also be created for specification. For details, contact the Sales Director at the address above.

dedication

A growing body of evidence indicates that eating foods rich in omega-3 fatty acids, such as seafood, may help maintain cardiovascular health by playing a role in the regulation of blood clotting and vessel constriction. In other words, experts are now saying what the McCormick & Schmick's staff has known for a long time: Seafood is good for you!

In our Special Edition cookbook, we've added a new section with recipes focused on healthy eating—from Grilled Salmon with Strawberry & Blueberry Sauce to Swordfish Siciliana, these recipes were created especially for our guests to enjoy cooking at home. Using the freshest ingredients available is a revered tradition in our restaurants, and we are excited to pass that tradition on. It's the smart thing to do for your mind and for your body.

We would like to dedicate this edition of the *McCormick & Schmick's Seafood Restaurant Cookbook* to the thousands of loyal guests who have graciously made our restaurants their favorite dining destination. We appreciate your patronage.

Here's to your health,

Doug Schmick
CEO

table of contents

introduction

Since teaming up in the early 70s, Bill McCormick and Doug Schmick have established a number of individualized, finer-dining restaurants throughout the country. Combining their unique and extraordinary entrepreneurial talents into one collective vision, they have created the nation's premier family of seafood restaurants.

During the early years of Bill and Doug's partnership, the entire restaurant industry was in its infancy. There were no proven business models to follow, no courses or college programs in hotel and restaurant management available. That is to say, no one really knew anything about restaurant marketing. "So, all of us who got started at that time were just people who really loved what we were doing," says Doug. "We were having fun. Every night business was a little better. We all just kind of grew with the momentum of things and truly learned a lot."

The successful restaurant management model Bill and Doug created is based on doing things the old-fashioned way. Their approach emphasizes classic simplicity and downplays pretension.

The culture of McCormick & Schmick's is characterized by a strong commitment to quality food, a comfortable atmosphere, and excellent

> ## "I like nothing better than being a good host."
> —Bill McCormick

service. The key to their culinary success is a fresh approach to dining. "From a culinary perspective, straightforwardness and attention to the quality of ingredients is more important than just a creative and attractive presentation," says Doug. "There was a time when a lot of the food trends were such that some people would use creativity for creativity's sake. The reality was that there were a lot of things that didn't really have any substance to them. They might look artful, but they really weren't substantive."

McCormick & Schmick's purposefully steers away from trendiness. That's not to say that their food isn't progressive or isn't bringing in a variety of influences. "Fundamentally," says Doug, "we still really believe in the tradition of a great piece of fresh fish, perfectly cooked vegetables, and flavorful rice or potatoes."

Seafood is still the main focus of the McCormick & Schmick's family of restaurants, and only the freshest ingredients will do. Each restaurant's chef strives to reflect McCormick & Schmick's commitment to culinary excellence by showcasing an array of the highest quality specialties from the Pacific Northwest and the waters of the Atlantic, as well as prime selections from the Gulf of Mexico and other exotic waters around the world. McCormick & Schmick's chefs explore the rich possibilities inherent in the natural bounty by preparing dishes that enhance the natural flavors of the food.

Community awareness is reflected in the restaurants' menu. Each restaurant has a unique culinary approach centered around a core selection of about fifty recipes designed to appear on every restaurant menu. Daily menus announcing the "fresh list" are presented to guests who must then decide from a myriad of culinary delights. Frequent patrons know whatever they select will be both eye-catching and tasteful.

"At least thirty percent of the menu items are very reflective of what the local community is all about," says Bill. He and Doug encourage individual restaurants to respect the local palates and preferences of their diners. They hope to strike a balance between their Pacific Northwest heritage and regional expression, on the menu, in the décor, and in the ambiance.

At McCormick & Schmick's, rich mahogany, copper-top tables, and stained-glass windows create an ambiance of timeless tradition. Whether located in a historic property or a more contemporary building, every restaurant emphasizes tradition and comfort, creating an inviting, original, and relaxing atmosphere. Like the cities in which they are located, each restaurant has its own style, local appeal, and story.

Through their own stories, Bill and Doug will tell you that the real secret to opening a successful restaurant is to have the everyday customer feel comfortable and welcome, while at the same time creating a truly social, interactive, and fun environment. "It's such a colorful business because when people go to a restaurant, it's a different experience than going shopping," says Bill. "They're not going to a department or grocery store; they're going out for an event. They dress up to look good... and they do look good! We try to provide the quality environment and event that assures they feel good too." This strong commitment to service is obvious when you visit any one of their restaurants. Customers are served by knowledgeable, helpful, and people-oriented staff in a very attractive and comfortable environment. McCormick & Schmick's has an unparalleled reputation for excellence in service in the restaurant and hospitality industry.

> "We still really believe in the tradition of a great piece of fresh fish, perfectly cooked vegetables, and flavorful rice or potatoes."
>
> -Doug Schmick

"Establishing a restaurant and running it well requires the creative imagination and stamina that go into producing a Broadway play," says Schmick. "Over the years, the hardest thing conceptually was to change with the times and remain a force in the industry without straying from what made this company so successful in the first place." Making it work are the company's leaders and employees, including some of the finest chefs in the world.

As a deliberate extension of their restaurant philosophy, Bill and Doug hope that the McCormick & Schmick's Seafood Restaurant Cookbook will become a treasured classic in your culinary library.

seafood:
making a splash

Bill McCormick and Doug Schmick have achieved their vision of running the nation's premier family of seafood restaurants. Not known for resting on their laurels, the dynamic duo has now brought their love of seafood to the Internet with their passionate message about the health benefits of eating seafood. In March of 2008, they launched their new consumer education web site, SeafoodHealth.com.

Hungry for Resources
"Continually, more studies and organizations like the American Heart Association and the USDA are recommending and encouraging consumers to eat more seafood as part of a healthy diet," says Doug Schmick, chairman and CEO. He adds that today's consumers are hungry for as many resources as they can find on healthy dining and healthy lifestyles.

Schmick states that, as a national leader in the seafood industry for the past thirty-six years, it is their company's responsibility to educate consumers about the power of seafood as one of the healthiest proteins available. The Internet is a natural place to do this as it enables us to reach a large audience and update them quickly. "Creating SeafoodHealth.com helped us to do just that," Schmick explains.

Eat Seafood Twice a Week
The American Heart Association recommends that consumers eat at least two servings of seafood each week to promote a healthy lifestyle. The National Institutes of Health believes that the omega-3 fatty acids found in seafood reduces the risk of heart attack and other cardiovascular diseases. Other health experts have weighed in, such as *The Journal of the American Medical Association,* indicating that the modest consumption of fish reduces the risk of coronary death by 36 percent.

Easy-to-Prepare Recipes
"Many people are intimidated by preparing seafood at home, and we want to help show them how easy and healthy it can be. We want to provide a wide variety of seafood recipes that are easy to prepare at home. Our chefs across the country have

supplied some delicious, healthy and simple recipes that will be featured on the site each week," notes Schmick.

Seafood for a Healthy Heart

Recent studies show that increased seafood consumption can have many positive effects on our health. In fact, the American Heart Association recommends eating fish for better health.

The Journal of the American Medical Association found that modest consumption of fish reduces risk of coronary death by 36 percent. Researchers found that the health benefits of eating seafood outweigh the potential risks.

Omega-3 in Fish: How Eating Fish Helps Your Heart

Two federally sponsored studies have also concluded that eating fish can help your heart and reduce your risk of dying from a heart attack by a third or more.

Tufts Researchers Find That Omega-3s Can Reduce Risk Of Cardiovascular Disease: Research associates at Tufts-New England Medical Center concluded that by increasing your consumption of omega-3s, you can "reduce the rates of all-cause mortality, cardiac and sudden death, and possibly stroke."

Heart-Health Benefits of Omega-3s: Research has found that omega-3s can help survivors of heart attacks reduce their risk of mortality from heart disease by one half, in comparison to those who do not consume these essential fatty acids.

Moderate Fish Consumption May Reduce Risk of Sudden Cardiac Death: Research published in the *Journal of the American College of Cardiology* also found that moderate consumption of fish rich in omega-3s seems to have a direct effect on the heart's electrical function, which determines the rate at which the heart beats. By eating fish once or twice a week, we may help to lower the resting heart rate and slow the time between beats, thereby reducing the risk of sudden cardiac death.

Healthy Body

Fish Oil May Help Ease Back Pain: In addition to being good for your heart, seafood consumption has also been found to address other body ailments. Recent research shows that omega-3 fatty acids can be a safe alternative for alleviating these aches and pains.

Specifically, a recent study shows that fish-oil supplements containing omega-3 fatty acids might help treat neck and back pain. Such supplements might be "a safer alternative" to non-steroidal anti-inflammatory drugs for some patients with spine-related pain.

Study: Omega-3 fatty acids may help reduce the risks of diabetes:
Researchers have recently revealed that children with a family history of diabetes can lower their risk of developing the disease by eating foods rich in omega-3 fatty acids.

Healthy Mind
Eating Fish May Help with Depression:
Eating seafood isn't only a smart idea for your body; it's beneficial to your mind. Studies show that people who eat seafood may be less likely to suffer from bipolar disorder and it may also help people battle depression.

Studies have shown that fish oil may make significant improvements on mental health. The active ingredients in fish oil are needed for the brain to function properly and have good overall health. Primarily, fish oil works well in stabilizing the mood because the brain needs fatty acids to function properly. When the brain doesn't have the appropriate fatty acids and vitamins it needs, depression and other disorders may occur in the brain. Omega-3 fatty acids may help the brain function properly because it is believed to provide a stabilizing effect. But new research shows that one nutrient in fish might actually be more effective in halting symptoms of depression than traditional antidepressants. The nutrient is an omega-3 fatty acid called EPA. In a recent article from *Psychology Today*, Willow Lawson wrote:

> *"British scientists recently gave a group of patients with stubborn depression a daily dose of EPA. After three months, over two-thirds of the group reported a 50 percent reduction in their symptoms—particularly feelings of sadness and pessimism, inability to work, sleeplessness and low libido.*
> *'This is one of the largest potential associations of a nutrient with depression,' says Joseph Hibbeln, M.D., a psychiatrist at the National Institutes of Health, who has long studied the diet-depression link. 'The important issue in this study is that the omega-3 worked above and beyond the antidepressants.'"*

Healthy Babies
Several studies have found that regular seafood consumption is an important part of a pregnant woman's diet because of the need for DHA omega-3, a critical nutrient for the development and health of a baby's brain, heart, and eyes. Additional studies have also shown that eating seafood while pregnant may increase the child's IQ and lead to better developmental skills. This study also found no evidence of harmful effects from eating fish for pregnant women.

The Fats of Life Newsletter focuses on the importance of essential fatty acids, Arachidonic acid (AA) and DHA, in fetal development. This article cites the extremely low consumption of fish by women in the United States and emphasizes that these essential fatty acids are important in fetal development in the brain cells, the vascular system, and other tissues as well.

Studies also show that eating fish during pregnancy can help prevent allergies and asthma. For women of childbearing age, benefits of modest fish intake outweigh potential risks, with the exception of a few selected species.

Healthy Seniors

Senior citizens' seafood-eating habits have been the target of several recent studies, and the results are in—fish consumption has many added benefits for seniors. Fish oils have been found to help prevent age-related cognitive decline, ease back pain, and protect against retinal degenerative diseases.

Recent research shows that omega-3 fatty acids in fish oil play a role in protecting cells in the retina from degenerative diseases like retinitis pigmentosa and age-related macular degeneration, the leading cause of vision loss in those older than sixty-five.

Dietary Recommendations

The American Heart Association recommends that you eat at least two servings of fish each week. (One serving equals about three ounces cooked, or a serving about the size of a checkbook). Fish, especially oily fish, is rich in omega-3 polyunsaturated fatty acids.

Food Pyramid

The 2005 dietary guidelines advise Americans to consume more fish to live "longer, healthier, and more active lives." The United States Department of Agriculture recommends that individuals over the age of two emphasize fruits, vegetables, whole grains, and fat-free or low-fat milk and milk products, as well as lean meats, poultry, fish, beans, eggs, and nuts in their diets. It also recommends a diet low in saturated fats or transfats, cholesterol, salt, and added sugars.

According to the USDA, some fish, (such as salmon, trout, and herrings) are high in omega fatty acids. It also states that there is some limited evidence suggesting that fish rich in omega-3 fatty acids may reduce the risk of mortality from cardiovascular disease.

*For more information on all of these topics, we invite you to visit **SeafoodHealth.com.***

"We are pleased to present some of these heart-healthy recipes in this special edition of our cookbook. Some of the dishes are served in McCormick & Schmick's restaurants, while others are recipes that our chefs enjoy preparing for their families and friends."

-DOUG SCHMICK

pan roasted
alaskan halibut WITH
green chili broth

The firm white meat and delicately sweet flavor of halibut, combined with the fact that it is a truly nutrient-dense food, makes this a winning choice for your health. A very good source of high-quality protein, halibut is rich in significant amounts of a variety of important nutrients and perhaps most important, the beneficial omega-3 essential fatty acids.

Yield: 4 servings

4 (7-ounce) portions Alaskan halibut
1/3 cup chopped yellow onion
2 tablespoons roasted garlic
2 tablespoons butter
5 ounces white wine
2/3 cup roasted red peppers
2/3 cup roasted yellow peppers
2/3 cup roasted poblano chilis

10 ounces fish stock
1/2 cup purple pearl onions
1 teaspoon salt
fi teaspoon freshly ground black pepper
2 tablespoons freshly chopped cilantro
2 tablespoons olive oil, for sautéing
4 cups cooked jasmine rice

For garnish:
Diced tomatoes
Lime wedges
Fresh cilantro leaves

Preheat the oven to 400°F.

Sauté the onions and garlic in the butter. Add the white wine and reduce until the pan is almost dry. Dice the roasted peppers and chilis and add to the pot along with the stock, pearl onions, salt and pepper. Simmer for 30 minutes. Strain the pepper mixture and purée one-fourth of the vegetables in a blender. Add everything back to pot, and add the cilantro. Season with more salt and pepper if necessary. Keep the sauce warm while you cook the fish.

Heat the olive oil in an oven-safe sauté pan until very hot. Season the halibut with salt and pepper. Carefully add the fish to the pan and cook for 30 seconds. Turn the fish with a spatula and place it in the oven. Cook for 4 to 6 minutes, depending on the thickness of the fish. Remove from pan.

To serve, place 1 cup of the cooked rice in the middle of each serving bowl. Fill each bowl with one-quarter of the broth and place the fish on top of the rice. Garnish with diced tomatoes, a lime wedge, and fresh cilantro leaves.

grilled salmon WITH strawberry & blueberry salsa

Eating this easy and delicious meal can actually help lower your cholesterol! Salmon affects HDL and LDL cholesterol, because it contains omega-3 fatty acids that increase HDL, or "good" cholesterol and decrease total cholesterol, LDL "bad" cholesterol, and triglycerides.

Yield: 2 servings

2 (6 to 8-ounce) salmon fillets
Salt
Freshly ground black pepper

Berry Salsa
1 cup blueberries
1 cup diced strawberries
1 tablespoon finely chopped red onion
1 tablespoon finely chopped red bell pepper
1 teaspoon finely chopped jalapeño pepper
1 ounce freshly squeezed lime juice
1 ounce extra virgin olive oil
1 ounce balsamic vinegar
1/2 teaspoon cumin
2 tablespoons finely chopped cilantro
Olive oil
Salt
Freshly ground black pepper

To make the salsa, combine all the ingredients, and mix well.

Drizzle the salmon with a little olive oil and season with salt and pepper. Sear in a hot pan until desired doneness.

Serve the salmon topped with the salsa.

pistachio crusted salmon

Not only is salmon rich in omega-3 fatty acids and a great start to a super-healthy meal, pistachios also contain heart-healthy fat, and overall, they have a very good nutritional profile. According to the California Pistachio Commission, a one-ounce serving of pistachios—about forty-seven nuts—provides more fiber than a half cup of spinach and the same amount as an orange or apple.

Yield: 2 servings

2 (5-ounce) salmon fillets
1/3 cup pistachios
1/8 teaspoon cayenne pepper
2 tablespoons freshly chopped cilantro
Olive-oil spray, or olive oil

Preheat the oven to 350°F.

Place the pistachios, cayenne pepper, and cilantro into a food processor. Pulse several times to coarsely chop the nuts. Pour the mixture into a shallow bowl. Mist the salmon with olive-oil spray, or brush them lightly with olive oil. Press the flesh-side of the salmon into the nut mixture, turning as necessary to fully coat.

Prepare an oven-safe pan with olive-oil spray and place the salmon in the pan. Roast for 15 to 20 minutes, or until the fish flakes easily.

seared cod WITH artichoke piccata

Cod has been shown to be one of the best meat sources in terms of reducing atherosclerosis and heart disease in those who have diabetes. Those consuming cod as a regular part of their diet also have a decreased risk of heart attack and show a greater likelihood of meeting their vitamin B12 needs, as cod is high in that nutrient as well.

Yield: 4 servings

2 (6 to 7-ounce) cod fillets
Salt
Freshly ground black pepper
/ cup light olive oil
1 tablespoon minced garlic
1/2 cup artichoke hearts, quartered
1/8 cup chopped kalamata olives
1/8 cup diced tomatoes
1 tablespoon capers
1/2 cup roasted red potatoes
3 ounces white wine
3 ounces chicken stock
2 tablespoons freshly-squeezed lemon juice
2 tablespoons unsalted butter

Season the cod with salt and pepper and cook to desired doneness on a grill or in a sauté pan. Heat the olive oil in a sauté pan and add the garlic. Sauté until golden. Add the artichoke hearts, olives, tomatoes, capers, and potatoes. Sauté for 2 to 3 minutes to heat through.

Add the wine and reduce by half. Add the chicken stock and reduce by half. Add the lemon juice and butter, and cook until a thickened sauce forms.

Place the sauce in middle of a serving plate. Place the fish on top and serve!

rs

We know that the typical family meal is not a multi-course event. Still, there are many meals that do call for a first course. The recipes in this section will give you a variety of choices for when you wish to kick off your meal with style.

crab, mango, & avocado salad

This is an easy and elegant start for a special meal. But it is also an excellent "stand alone" for a light lunch or supper if made a little larger. The key is to build a "tower" or "stack" using a ring mold (available in specialty cookware stores) to form the salad. If you cannot find the pomegranate reduction at a specialty or Asian-foods store, use a light syrup.

Yield: 4 servings

3/4 cup diced mango
3/4 cup diced avocado
10 ounces Dungeness crab
4 tablespoons pomegranate reduction
4 tablespoons citrus-flavored vinaigrette
4 tablespoons chive oil (page 113)
1/2 cup micro greens or spicy sprouts tossed in
    a small amount of the citrus vinaigrette, for garnish

To create the "tower," place a 2-inch ring mold on a serving plate. Spoon 2 heaping tablespoons of diced mango into the mold. Layer 2 heaping tablespoons of avocado on top of the mango. Finish with 1 1/2 ounces of crab meat to fill the mold. Press down lightly to set the ingredients. Keeping your fingers or a spoon on top of the tower, apply pressure, and gently slide the ring mold up and off of the salad. Rinse and dry the mold before moving on to the remaining plates.

Garnish the top of each salad with the micro greens. Drizzle pomegranate reduction, citrus vinaigrette, and chive oil on the plate and around the tower.

dungeness crab & bay shrimp cakes

This recipe and the next are companion recipes for our ever-popular Crab Cakes. We take advantage of the opportunity to utilize the two species of crab that are most prevalent in the United States: Dungeness, on the West Coast and blue crab, available on the East Coast. Both are wonderful, but produce distinctively different results. Dungeness is sweeter and more delicate, while blue crab is more rich and buttery. We avoid the debate over which is best, and suggest you try both and then decide for yourself.

Yield: 12 cakes, 6 servings

3/4 pounds Dungeness crab meat
3/4 pounds bay shrimp
3 tablespoons chopped celery
3 tablespoons chopped onion
3 tablespoons mayonnaise
1 egg, beaten
Pinch cayenne pepper
Pinch dry mustard
2 tablespoons Dijon mustard, smooth
1 tablespoon Worcestershire sauce

Pinch of salt
Pinch of pepper
Pinch of Old Bay seasoning
1/2 cup Panko bread crumbs
3 ounces freshly squeezed lemon juice
Vegetable oil, for frying
Lemon wedges, for garnish
Fresh parsley sprigs, for garnish
Tartar sauce (page 181)

Make sure that the crab and bay shrimp are both well drained and dry. If necessary, squeeze them slightly to extract the excess water. Grind the celery and the onion in a food processor. Place the ground celery and onions in a large bowl and add the shrimp, mayonnaise, eggs, cayenne, dry mustard, Dijon mustard, Worcestershire sauce, salt, pepper, and Old Bay seasoning. Add in three-quarters of the Panko bread crumbs and blend. Fold in the crab. *Do not over-mix.* Form into 4-ounce patties. Place on a sheet pan or cookie sheet and sprinkle with the remaining Panko. Let the cakes refrigerate for at least an hour, but no more than 2 to 3 hours. These cakes can be deep-fried, pan-fried, or lightly drizzled with oil and baked in a 400°F oven. Serve with tartar sauce and garnish with lemon and parsley. If deep frying, fry until cakes are a deep golden brown; if pan frying, fry 3 to 4 minutes per side, until the cakes are a deep golden brown.

blue crab cakes

*The cooking process for this crab species is the same as for Dungeness, but the results are very different. These cakes are chock-full of crab meat and are absolutely **terrific!***

Yield: 6 servings (12 cakes)

1/4 cup mayonnaise
1/2 cup pasteurized eggs
1/2 tablespoon Old Bay seasoning
1/2 tablespoon coarsely ground black pepper
1/2 tablespoon dry mustard
1/2 teaspoon salt
1 teaspoon Worcestershire sauce
1/2 loaf white bread, crust removed, and diced to about 1/4 inch
2 pounds blue crab meat
3 tablespoons chopped fresh parsley

Use only fresh crab meat, not pasteurized meat. Combine mayonnaise, eggs, Old Bay seasoning, black pepper, dry mustard, salt, and Worcestershire sauce in a bowl to form a sauce base. Mix the bread, crab meat, and parsley in a separate bowl. Gently fold the sauce into the crab meat mixture. *Be careful not to break up the crab.* The mixture must be made at least 2 hours before forming into crab cakes so that the bread will absorb the liquid. Once chilled, portion into 4-ounce cakes. Chill before cooking.

These cakes can be deep-fried, pan-fried, or lightly drizzled with oil and baked in a 400°F oven. Serve with tartar sauce and garnish with lemon and parsley. If deep frying, fry until cakes are a deep golden brown; if pan-frying, fry 3 to 4 minutes per side, until the cakes are a deep golden brown.

crab tater tots

*This one will bring out the child in everyone.
Amaze your guests with homemade tater tots—
filled with crab, no less. The yield may seem like
a large amount, but trust us—they go fast.*

Yield: 80 to 100 tots—approximately 10 servings

1 pound cream cheese
3 tablespoons minced garlic
1/4 cup chopped fresh
   cilantro
1/4 cup chopped green onion
1 tablespoon Chipotle pepper
   purée
1/4 cup cream

1 cup shredded mild cheddar
   cheese
1/2 tablespoon Tabasco sauce
1 pound crab meat
1 pound bay shrimp
3 pounds shredded, frozen
   hash-brown potatoes
3 cups Panko bread crumbs

Allow the cream cheese to soften at room temperature for about an hour before making the tots. Blend the cream cheese with an electric mixer until smooth. Fold in the remaining ingredients and blend thoroughly. To form the tots, pinch off a generous tablespoon of the mixture and roll into a ball. Mold into a "tater tot" shape by gently squeezing the sides of the ball to form the traditional cylindrical shape.

These are best deep-fried, but they can be drizzled with oil and baked at 400°F for 10 to 12 minutes. Whichever cooking method you use, the tots must be very cold before cooking, so refrigerate them for at least 1 to 2 hours. (They can even be frozen. Allow them to thaw, refrigerated for 1 to 2 hours.)

Chef's note: Serve these with your favorite dipping sauce. We use tartar sauce spiked with jalapeño peppers.

seafood cocktails

Seafood Cocktails have been a mainstay of fine restaurant menus since long before any of us can remember, and with good reason. Whether using crab meat, jumbo prawns, or tiny pink bay shrimp, the result will be a sweet and fresh-tasting appetizer enhanced by a lively cocktail sauce.

Yield: 2 servings

6 to 8 ounces fresh Dungeness crab meat, *or*
6 to 8 ounces fresh bay shrimp, *or*
12 jumbo prawns, peeled and deveined
4 tablespoons cocktail sauce (page 175)
Crushed ice
Shredded iceberg lettuce
Lemon wedge, for garnish

If you're making prawn cocktails, cook the prawns in simmering water or white wine or a combination of both, and flavor the mixture with a squeeze of lemon and a pinch of pickling spice. Drain and chill.

The classic seafood cocktail is served in a pedestal supreme dish designed to hold crushed ice in its base while the seafood sits on top, where it is chilled, but not watered down by the ice. Since most of us don't stock such items in our homes, a nice arrangement can be made by placing a small dish on a nicely folded napkin on a larger plate. Surround the dish with crushed ice, spreading it over the folded napkin. Then put the plates in the freezer until you're ready to serve.

When you're ready to serve, remove the frozen plates. Put some of the shredded lettuce in the dish with a tablespoon of cocktail sauce. Arrange the seafood on top and finish with another spoonful of sauce. Serve a lemon wedge on the side.

Chef's note: Don't worry about the ice melting all over your table. It doesn't take that long to eat a great crab cocktail, and the little ice that may melt will be absorbed by the napkin.

portobello, mozzarella, & tomato bruschetta

Bruschetta, toasted slices of crusty bread topped with your favorite meats, cheeses, vegetables or seafood, are always crowd pleasers. Whether for a sit-down first course or a party hors d'oeuvre, this one is simple and classic.

Yield: 12 Bruschetta

12 slices of baguette
3 Portobello mushrooms
12 slices of fresh mozzarella
1 cup chopped, assorted tomatoes
3 tablespoons Extra virgin olive oil
3 tablespoons chopped fresh basil
1 ounce balsamic syrup
1 ounce Extra virgin olive oil

Toss the assorted tomatoes with 3 tablespoons of olive oil and the chopped basil. Set aside.

Drizzle the baguette slices with olive oil and toast under the broiler. Grill the Portobello (recipe below). Place a slice of Portobello mushroom on each baguette slice. Top each with a slice of fresh mozzarella. Briefly bake or broil the bruschetta to melt the cheese. Remove from the oven and place on a serving platter. Top each one with a tablespoon of the prepared tomatoes. Drizzle the ounce of olive oil and the balsamic syrup over the bruschetta.

Grilled Portobello:
Coat Portobello with olive oil and season with salt and pepper. Grill or roast until done. When done, the mushrooms should be browned and "spongy" to the touch, yet firm. Slice mushrooms 1/4-inch thick by 3-inches long and 1/2-inch wide.

seared rare ahi

*Yellowfin tuna, or ahi, is best when served raw or, as in this recipe, seared **very** rare. The tuna must be **perfectly** fresh, so be sure to purchase it from a seafood market that you trust. This is one of the most popular items on our menu.*

Yield: 2 servings

1 (5-ounce) yellowfin tuna steak
Cajun spice, to taste
3 ounces soy sauce
2 tablespoons wasabi
2 tablespoons pickled ginger
1/2 cup Asian Cucumber Salad (recipe below)

Dust the tuna lightly with the Cajun spice. Briefly sear the steak in a very hot pan coated with a tablespoon of oil (5 to 10 seconds *only* on all sides). Allow the tuna to cool for a minute, then carefully slice the steak into 10 to 12 pieces.

Toss the ingredients for the Asian Cucumber Salad (recipe below). Lay the ahi slices decoratively on two plates and garnish with the remaining ingredients.

Asian Cucumber Salad:
1 average-sized cucumber, peeled, seeded, and thinly sliced
2 tablespoons thinly sliced red bell pepper
2 tablespoons thinly sliced red onion
2 tablespoons sweet Thai chili sauce
Pinch of sugar
2 to 3 tablespoons rice wine vinegar
If desired, a small amount of chopped seaweed, like wakame, may be added.

steamed mussels in red curry sauce

A little spicy, a little sweet, and a little rich,
*these mussels are **a lot** delicious!*
As a bonus, they are quick and easy!

Yield: 2 servings

Curry Base:
3 tablespoons vegetable oil
5 tablespoons red curry paste
2 cups canned coconut milk

To prepare the curry base, sauté the curry paste in hot oil. Add the coconut milk and bring to a boil. Set aside.

For the mussels:
2 tablespoons clarified butter (page 175)
2 tablespoons chopped garlic
2 tablespoons chopped shallots
20 ounces black mussels
1/2 cup Roma tomatoes, diced to about 1/2 inch
1/2 cup chicken stock
1 1/2 cups prepared curry base (recipe above)
1 tablespoon freshly squeezed lime juice

Sauté the garlic and shallots in the butter. Add the mussels and tomatoes. Toss well. Add the chicken stock, curry base, and lime juice. Cover and steam until the mussels are open. Pour mussels into bowls and arrange them with the open ends facing up.

crab rangoon

These wonderful wraps really need to be deep-fried or pan-fried in deep oil, techniques which can be a little tricky at home. However, the results are well worth the trouble. Like many of our appetizers, these rangoons are perfect as a first course or as an hors d'oeuvre.

Yield: 16 pieces

1/2 pound cream cheese, softened
1/2 pound crab meat
1 tablespoon A-1 Sauce
1/2 teaspoon onion powder
1/2 teaspoon garlic powder
Pinch of salt
Pinch of pepper

16 (4-inch by 4-inch) won ton wrappers
1/4 cup yellow cornmeal
2 egg yolks, mixed with 2 tablespoons water
2 cups vegetable oil
1 cup Cashew Dipping Sauce (page 174)

Beat the cream cheese with an electric mixer until soft and smooth. Fold in the crab meat, the A-1 Sauce, and the spices, and blend. *Do not over-mix.* Scatter the cornmeal on a cookie sheet or on your work surface. Arrange the won ton wrappers at the front of your work area. Place a generous tablespoon of the crab filling in the center of each wrapper, leaving a border around the filling. Moisten the edges of each won ton with the egg mixture. Fold the wrapper over onto itself, corner to corner, to form a triangle. Pinch the two opposite corners together to form the rangoon shape. Make sure all the seams are sealed well. Chill the rangoons for at least 1 to 2 hours, or overnight.

To cook: heat the oil in a deep pan to between 350°F and 360°F, using a candy thermometer. Fry the rangoons until crisp and golden, about 2 to 3 minutes.

assorted sashimi

The popularity of sushi, sashimi, and raw seafood in general is growing rapidly in the United States. Here is a very nice combination of ideal sashimi fish that our guests rave about. This dish is a perfect first course or, in larger quantities, party platter. The keys are fresh fish and an artful eye for presentation.

Yield: 2 servings

4 slices salmon fillet 1 1/2 inches by 3 inches
4 slices Hamachi (yellowtail) 1 1/2 inches by 3 inches
4 slices ahi tuna, 1 1/2 inch by 3 inches
3-inch by 6-inch nori sheet
1/4 red bell pepper, thinly sliced
1/2 avocado, sliced and "fanned"
2 tablespoons pickled ginger
2 tablespoons wasabi paste
1/2 cup Asian Cucumber Salad (page 173)
2 ounces soy sauce

Arrange all three fish on your plate. Using the nori sheet as a decorative underliner, garnish the plate with the remaining ingredients. Finish the plate with a ramekin of soy sauce.

crab, shrimp, & artichoke dip

Want to please a crowd? This dip is perfect for any party!
It is truly best with the blue crab from the East Coast,
but Dungeness is certainly an acceptable substitute.

Yield: 8 generous servings

3/4 cup cream cheese
1/4 cup Dijon mustard
1/3 cup mayonnaise
2 teaspoons Old Bay Seasoning
1/2 teaspoon garlic powder
1 cup coarsely chopped artichoke hearts
3/4 pound blue crab meat
3/4 pound bay shrimp
80 pieces fried pita, crustini, or tortilla chips
1/2 cup pico de gallo, for garnish

Beat the cream cheese with an electric mixer for 1 to 2 minutes until smooth. Combine the mustard, mayonnaise, and seasonings, and blend thoroughly. Fold in the artichokes, the crab and the shrimp. *Do not over-mix.* Bake the mixture in a casserole dish and serve with crustini, fried pita chips, or tortilla chips. Optionally, you may try melting shredded cheese on top of the casserole or even over the chips for added color and flavor. Garnish the top of the casserole with the pico de gallo.

panchetta-wrapped prawns

Prawns and shrimp are really the same species in the United States. For this recipe, select the largest shrimp you can find—ideally U-12s, which means that there are fewer than 12 shrimp per pound. These are the biggest shrimp generally available.

Yield: 12 pieces

12 large prawns, peeled and deveined
12 thinly sliced panchetta
1/2 cup Asian barbecue sauce (recipe below)
1/2 cup finely diced Roma tomatoes
4 tablespoons finely chopped red, green, and yellow peppers
1 tablespoon chopped fresh cilantro

3 tablespoons chopped green onions
1/2 teaspoon minced garlic
1 tablespoon chunky peanut butter
1 tablespoon chili paste with garlic or sambal oelek
4 tablespoons chopped, salted cocktail peanuts
1 sprig fresh cilantro, for garnish

Wrap each prawn with panchetta and grill both sides until the panchetta is browned. Coat the prawns with the Asian barbecue sauce. Combine the tomatoes, peppers, chopped cilantro, chopped green onions, garlic, peanut butter, chili paste, and peanuts to make a peanut salsa. Place 1/4 cup of salsa in the center of each plate, and arrange the prawns around the salsa. Garnish with a sprig of cilantro.

Asian Barbecue Sauce:

2 cups plum sauce
1/4 cup hoisin sauce
1/4 cup freshly squeezed orange juice

2 tablespoons chopped fresh cilantro
Pinch of crushed red chili flakes

Combine all ingredients and blend thoroughly. This sauce is best when prepared a day in advance.

gazpacho shrimp cocktail

This is a very festive and refreshing appetizer. The hot, grilled shrimp and the cool gazpacho and avocado salad complement each other perfectly.

Yield: 4 servings

4 (6 to 8-inch) bamboo skewers
20 medium-size shrimp
2 tablespoons vegetable oil
2 tablespoons Southwest seasoning
2 cups Gazpacho (page 176)
1 cup Avocado Salsa (page 173)
6 to 8 tortilla chips (various colors, if available)
1 sprig of fresh cilantro for each serving, for garnish

Soak the bamboo skewers in water for several hours before using. Thread 5 shrimp on each skewer. Coat the shrimp with the vegetable oil and dust with a Southwest seasoning, and grill for 2 minutes on each side.

Pour the Gazpacho into 4 medium Margarita glasses. Mound the Avocado Salsa in the center of each glass. Lay the skewer across the Avocado Salsa mound. Garnish with a sprig of cilantro. Scatter the tortilla chips around the base of the glass.

oysters
ON THE HALF SHELL

THERE ARE FEW DINING EXPERIENCES so closely related to the sea as a freshly opened oyster on the half shell. There are also few other seafoods, or foods of any kind for that matter, so immersed in history and romance.

From the time of the Roman Empire two thousand years ago, man has been captivated by this exalted member of the mollusk family. Much has been written and, in recent years, sophisticated oyster culture has taught us a great deal about proper care and handling.

Although Roman legions did collect and transplant oysters near the mouth of the Adriatic Sea before the birth of Christ, it is the Japanese who are generally credited with the development of oyster culture in the early seventeenth century. The Japanese connection proved critical to the Pacific Northwest's oyster industry, which three hundred years later was trying to rebound from disastrous over-harvesting of the indigenous Olympic oyster in the nineteenth century. In an attempt to satisfy the enormous demands of the Gold Rush Era of San Francisco, the industry had almost self-destructed.

Willapa Bay, Washington, then known as Shoalwater Bay, had been the repository of a seemingly unlimited supply of the tiny, coppery Olympias. The species was a staple of the Chinook Indian's diet for centuries, but insatiable demand had all but rendered them extinct.

Then along came the Japanese seed or "spat" and oystermen with common sense and a respect for the Northwest's great natural assets. Slowly the eradication began to reverse. In the last three decades, growers trained in marine biology who were willing to experiment with revolutionary oyster culture techniques established themselves, and oyster cultivation became state of the art. Now, Willapa Bay, along with bays and inlets from Northern California to Southeastern Alaska, produce some of the world's finest oysters. Olympias are truly one of the premier products the region has to offer.

It helps to know your oysters. There's nothing wrong with an "ignorance is bliss" approach to oyster experimentation, but once your passion for them has been established, you'll want to know the subtleties of flavor imparted by each oyster bed location. Words like coppery, smokey-sweet, and cucumber-scented are the vernacular of oyster experts whose discussions sometimes get a little too intellectual for our taste. The best way to get to know your oysters is to try them firsthand. Here are a few tips to make your oyster tasting a success.

TYPES OF OYSTERS

There are four basic varieties of oysters grown in the Pacific Northwest: the tiny Olympia, which is no bigger than a quarter and is unique to our region; the European Flat, which is a variation on the French Belon and similar to most East Coast and Gulf of Mexico varieties; the Kumamoto, which is generally the mildest, most delicate species and, as a result, is a good choice for beginners; and the Pacific which is by far the most prominent, and varies in size, shape, and flavor, depending upon where it is grown.

Some of the better Pacific oysters come from Shoalwater Bay, Westcott Bay, Quilcene, Hood Canal, and Penn Cove, but there are dozens of other growers in British Columbia and along the Northern California, Oregon, and Washington coasts producing fine quality oysters. There are also outstanding oysters being raised along the Atlantic Coast, from Nova Scotia to the Carolinas. The indigenous species is the Virginica, which is often large (5 to 6 inches) and full-flavored. In addition, the European Flats and Kumamotos are also being developed with great success.

SIZE

Although each variety is unique in size and shape, young oysters, which are smaller, are best for half-shell eating. Olympias can range up to 1 1/2 inches, European Flats, up to 4 to 5 inches, Pacifics, from 2 1/2 to 4 inches.

QUALITY AND FRESHNESS

It is impossible to assess an oyster's quality until you've looked inside. Ask your fishmonger to open one for you to inspect. If he is reluctant to do so, you're buying your oysters from the wrong person. You want to see lots of liquid inside the shell and plump, clear, bright-looking meat.

If the oyster's shell is cracked or damaged around its edges, don't buy it. The same goes for when the shell is open or gaping even slightly. Any of these characteristics is a sure sign of moisture loss and lack of quality and freshness, the by-products of poor handling.

Ask for the harvest date of the oysters before buying. (Stores are required to keep these records.) If the oysters have been out of water more than ten days, don't buy them. They may not be spoiled, but their quality will have deteriorated over time.

STORAGE AND HANDLING

If possible, oysters should be positioned with their deepest, cupped side down at all times. Doing so ensures moisture retention. When you get them home, scrub them with a brush under cold running water and store them under a damp cloth in the coldest part of your refrigerator. If purchased shortly after they were harvested, they should keep for several days; however, like all seafood, the fresher the better.

OPENING

If you are right-handed, put a kitchen towel in your left hand (if you're left-handed, reverse these directions). Place the oyster on a second, dampened towel on the counter in front of you with the pointed, hinged end pointing to your right. Cover the oyster with your toweled left hand, holding it firmly in place. Insert the point of the oyster knife into the hinge and twist the knife to release the top shell. Slide the knife along the inside of the top shell to separate the connector muscle and remove the top.

Take care not to tip the oyster, or you'll lose the precious liquid we've talked so much about. If there is no liquid, and the oyster looks dry and shriveled, discard it. Even among the best oysters, an occasional one loses its luster.

Once you've decided to eat the oyster, slide the knife under the oyster meat and sever the other connector muscle. Wipe any loose shell, sand, or other debris away with a clean finger.

SERVING

Serve the oysters on a bed of crushed ice. The best way is to place a decoratively folded napkin on a serving plate and put the ice on the napkin. The napkin will absorb what little ice melts. Accompany the oyster with a wedge of lemon and a little mignonette or cocktail sauce (pages 162).

pan-fried
oysters

The key to great pan-fried oysters, aside from using only quality specimens, is to fry them crisp. The oil must be hot and deep enough to almost deep-fry them in the pan. This method also applies to the oysters for the Po' Boy recipe (page 43).

Yield: 2 servings

10 to 12 shucked oysters (Use the smallest available.)
Flour, seasoned with salt and pepper, to coat
1 1/2 cup vegetable oil
1 cup shredded iceberg lettuce
4 ounces Tartar sauce (page 181)
Fresh parsley, for garnish
Lemon wedges, for garnish

Heat the oil in a large sauté pan. The oil should be very hot—just to the smoking point. While the oil is heating, dust the oysters in the flour. Fry the oysters until crisp, usually 1 1/2 to 2 minutes per side. Drain the oysters on paper towels. Place the shredded iceberg lettuce on serving plates. Place the oysters on top of the lettuce. Serve with tartar sauce. Garnish with lemon and parsley.

soups &

salads

A wonderful meal can be made from nothing more than a bowl of soup and a fresh, flavorful salad—especially when the selections are as substantial as those offered in this section. Our chowders, published here for the first time, are among the most popular items on our menus throughout the country.

grilled shrimp & fruit salad

*This is the ultimate warm-weather salad. Very bright
and refreshing. Select your favorite fruit for the mixture.
We use three kinds of melon, red grapes, pineapple,
and mango.*

Yield: 1 serving

2 bamboo or metal skewers
10 medium shrimp, peeled and deveined
2 cups mixed fruit, diced to about 1 inch
1 cup chopped romaine lettuce
3 ounces Cilantro-Orange Dressing (page 175)
2 Belgian endive leaves
1 ounce mung bean sprouts
Pinch of black sesame seeds
1 sprig fresh cilantro, for garnish

If you are using bamboo skewers, soak them in water for several
hours. Thread 5 shrimp onto each skewer. Toss the fruit and
romaine in the Cilantro-Orange Dressing. Grill the skewered shrimp
for 2 minutes on each side while basting with the dressing.
Mound the fruit mixture along the plate. Garnish the salad with
the endive leaves. Lay the shrimp on top of the salad. Scatter with
sprouts, sesame seeds, and garnish with a sprig of cilantro.

shrimp & crab louis salad

This is the all-time classic seafood salad. It can be prepared with crab meat, shrimp, or a combination of the two. Although this was a West Coast original, this salad is popular throughout the country.

Yield: 1 serving

For each salad:
1/2 head shredded iceberg lettuce
4 ounces Thousand Island Dressing (page 181)
6 slices cucumber
6 black olives, pitted
4 tomato wedges
2 hard-boiled eggs, halved
4 1/2 ounces bay shrimp
1 1/2 ounces Dungeness or Lump blue crab
1 ounce Thousand Island dressing
1 lemon wedge, for garnish
2 sprigs parsley, for garnish

Pile the lettuce in the center of a serving plate. Arrange the cucumber slices, olives, eggs, and tomato wedges around the lettuce. Ladle 4 ounces of dressing over the lettuce. Arrange the shrimp and/or crab on top of the salad. Ladle 1 ounce of dressing on the seafood. Garnish with parsley and a lemon wedge.

southwest bay shrimp & avocado salad

Colorful and flavorful, this salad is the perfect choice for when you're in a "Southwestern mood."

Yield: 1 serving

6 ounces bay shrimp
1/2 cup Gazpacho (page 176)
2 tablespoons sherry vinegar
2 tablespoons Extra virgin olive oil
3/4 cup shredded iceberg lettuce
3/4 cup shredded red and green cabbage
1/4 cup Ranch dressing
1/2 cup Avocado Salsa (page 173)
1/2 cup Roasted Corn Salsa (page 179)
Southwest spice to dust
6 to 8 colorful tortilla chips
Fresh cilantro, to garnish

Pour the Gazpacho into bowl. Drizzle the vinegar and oil around and over the Gazpacho. Toss the cabbage and iceberg in Ranch Dressing and mound in the bowl. Mix the Avocado Salsa and the Roasted Corn Salsa together and mound on top of the cabbage and iceberg. Mound the bay shrimp on top and garnish with cilantro. Dust the salad with Southwestern spice. Arrange the tortilla chips around the bowl.

niçoise salad

*This salad originated in Nice, France (hence, the name).
It was prepared with processed, canned tuna. We give it
a contemporary "spin" by using great, fresh ahi and searing
it briefly. It makes a perfect lunch any time of the year,
but when the local tomatoes are fresh, it's at its best.*

Yield: 1 serving

2 red potatoes, halved and cooked
1/2 cup diced, mixed tomatoes
1 ounce blanched green beans
6 Kalamata olives, pitted
1 boiled egg, quartered
1/2 ounce basil oil
1/2 ounce Extra virgin olive oil
3 ounces ahi tuna, sliced
1/4 ounce micro greens (optional)

Place the potato halves in the center of the plate. Toss the
tomato salad, olives, and beans together with the oils. Place this
mixture on top of the potatoes. Sear the tuna for a few seconds on
each side, and slice. Place sliced tuna on top of the salad. Place
the quartered egg on each end of the plate. Optional: top with
microgreens.

maryland crab soup

A wonderful, rich vegetable soup garnished with the great blue crab from the Chesapeake is a terrific start to any meal. This one is hearty enough to make a lunch or light meal on its own.

Yield: 2 quarts

2 tablespoons butter
1 cup carrots, medium dice
1 cup onion, medium dice
3/4 cup celery, medium dice
4 cups water
1/2 cup fresh corn kernels
1/2 cup frozen peas
1/2 cup green beans, cut 1 inch, fresh or frozen
1/2 cup shredded cabbage
2 tablespoons Old Bay Seasoning
4 tablespoons crab stock or bouillon base
1 tablespoon Worcestershire sauce
1 cup canned, diced tomatoes
1 cup tomato purée
1 teaspoon freshly ground black pepper
1 1/2 cups peeled, diced potatoes

Sauté the carrots, onions, and celery in a large pot in butter until softened. Add water and bring to a boil. Add corn, peas, green beans, and cabbage and return to a boil. Reduce and simmer for 15 minutes. Add remaining ingredients and continue to simmer until potatoes are cooked. Salt and pepper to taste.

new england clam chowder

Traditional clam chowder is the mainstay of every seafood restaurant throughout the country. There are as many recipes for it as there are chefs. Here's our version.

Yield: 2 quarts

2 cups medium diced potatoes
4 strips sliced bacon, not particularly lean
4 tablespoons margarine
3/4 cup flour
1/4 cup diced carrots
1/4 cup diced onions
1/4 cup diced green peppers
1/4 cup diced celery
1 quart water
1 (8-ounce) can clam juice
1 1/2 pounds clams
1 cup cream
1/2 teaspoon thyme
1/4 teaspoon sage
1/4 teaspoon white pepper
1/4 teaspoon salt
Butter pats

Blanch the potatoes until just barely tender. Rinse under cold running water, drain, and set aside.

Sauté the bacon in a 4-quart sauce pan over medium heat until it is crisp and all bacon fat has been rendered. Remove the bacon from the pan, dice, and set aside.

Return grease to the pot along with half the margarine. Add flour and cook the roux on low heat for 3 to 4 minutes. Remove the roux from pot and set aside. Add remaining margarine to pot and sauté the carrots, onions, green peppers, and celery over low heat to soften. Return roux to pot, and add the water and clam juice. Raise the heat to high and cook, stirring frequently for 6 to 8 minutes, until thickened. Add clams, bacon, potatoes, seasonings, and cream. Simmer about 5 minutes.

Serve in chowder bowls and float a pat of butter on top of each serving.

seafood & corn chowder

This chowder recipe has its foundation in the traditional clam chowders of New England. We modify it a bit to include a variety of shellfish and roasted fresh corn, which adds a sweetness and texture that our guests love.

Yield: 2 quarts

2 ears unshucked yellow corn
6 strips finely chopped bacon
3 ounces butter
1/2 pound onion, diced to about 1/4 inch
2 ounces celery, diced to about 1/4 inch
3/4 tablespoon chopped garlic
3/4 tablespoon chopped shallots
3 ounces all-purpose flour
1 cup clam juice
2 cups water
2 ounces clam base

1/2 teaspoon bay leaves
2 tablespoons chopped fresh parsley
1/4 teaspoon dry thyme
1/2 teaspoon salt
1/2 teaspoon white pepper
3/4 pound potatoes, diced to about 1/2 inch
1 1/2 cups heavy cream
6 ounces bay shrimp
6 ounces chopped clams
6 ounces bay scallops

Place the corn on a baking sheet and roast in the oven at 375°F until the husk turns dark brown and the corn is golden brown. Render the bacon completely in a pot on the stove over medium-high heat. Cook the bacon until crisp.

Once the bacon is done, add the butter and melt completely. Add the celery, onions, garlic, and shallots, and cook until tender (10 minutes). Add the flour and stir well. Cook for 15 minutes to form a roux. Add the clam juice to temper the roux. Add the water. Cook for 15 additional minutes.

After the corn has cooled, cut the kernels from the cob. Add the clam base, potatoes, corn kernels, and all seasonings. Simmer, stirring frequently, for 30 minutes or until the potatoes are tender. Add the cream and seafood, and stir well.

es & pasta

There's nothing like a great sandwich—unless it is an equally great pasta dish. When our guests make their menu selections, pastas and sandwiches are at the top of their list for lunch and dinner. We offer items from these menu categories as options to full, multi-course meals. This variety is one of the hallmarks of our menu designs.

crab cake sandwich

Crab cakes are not only great appetizers or main courses; they make fabulous sandwiches. The crisper, the better. These treats have been the star attractions on seafood menus for generations.

Yield: one sandwich

1 (6-ounce) crab cake (page 4 or 5)
1 burger or potato bun
2 tablespoons tartar sauce (page 181), or purchased
1/2 cup shredded iceberg lettuce

Prepare the crab cake recipe from the Appetizer section. Lightly toast the bun and spread tartar sauce on each side. Place shredded lettuce on top of the crab cake. Serve with your favorite accompaniments.

yellowfin tuna burger

*Granted, there is nothing authentically Asian about
a tuna burger, but this is one of the best and most interesting
sandwiches we know of. The flavors in the tuna burger
are wonderful and balance out perfectly with
the wasabi and cucumber salad.*

Yield: 2 burgers

Burger mixture:

1 pound yellowfin (ahi) tuna

2 tablespoons minced onion

1 tablespoon minced pickled
ginger

1/2 tablespoon Asian chili paste

2 tablespoons soy sauce

1/2 teaspoon sesame oil

2 tablespoons mayonnaise

3 tablespoons Panko bread
crumbs

1/8 teaspoon salt

1/8 teaspoon pepper

For the sandwich:

2 whole wheat buns

4 tablespoons wasabi aïoli (page 182)

4 tablespoons Asian Cucumber Salad (page 173)

Pulse the tuna in a food processor briefly to create pea-sized
pieces. Blend the tuna with all remaining ingredients and form
into 8-ounce patties. Chill before cooking.

Lightly oil the burger patties and cook on a hot grill or in a sauté
pan for 3 to 4 minutes. Flip and finish for an additional 3 to 4
minutes.

Spread the bun with wasabi aïoli and place the burger on the bun.
Top the burger with the Asian Cucumber Salad. Serve with your
favorite accompaniments.

bronzed catfish sandwich

Unlike blackening, which can produce smoky and sometimes scary results in a home kitchen, bronzing is a less extreme method of cooking meat. We actually prefer the process of bronzing, as it gives the coating of the fish a spicier yet sweeter flavor than true blackening does. Catfish is authentic and ideal for this technique, as it is firm and stands up to all the seasoning.

Yield: 2 sandwiches

4 tablespoons mayonnaise
1 tablespoon chopped, pickled jalapeño peppers
Dash of freshly squeezed lemon juice
1 teaspoon chopped capers
Pinch of Cajun or blackening spice
2 (4-ounce) catfish fillets
3 tablespoons Cajun or Blackening spice
3 tablespoons vegetable oil
2 sandwich rolls
4 slices tomato
1/2 cup shredded iceberg lettuce
3 to 4 red onion rings

To make a Creole mayonnaise, combine the mayonnaise, jalapeño peppers, lemon juice, and capers and add a pinch of Cajun or blackening spice. Heat the oil in a sauté pan until smoky. Coat the fish with the Cajun spice and carefully place it in the hot pan. Cook until dark and bronzed in color, about 2 minutes. Turn the fish and repeat the cooking. Remove from heat and set aside.

Spread the rolls with the Creole mayonnaise. Place the fish on the rolls. Top with lettuce, tomato, and onion to complete the sandwich.

oyster po' boy

Once you get the hang of frying oysters, this is a snap!
Refer to our Pan-Fried Oysters recipe (page 23)
for the technique. Then, enjoy this Louisiana
street food treat!

Yield: 2 servings

2 (8-inch) sub rolls, soft
4 ounces tartar sauce (page 181)
2 cups shredded iceberg lettuce
8 (1/8-inch thick) tomato slices
12 shucked oysters, prepared for frying

Fry oysters until golden brown. Coat the inside of the bun with tartar sauce. Place the lettuce and tomato slices on the roll. Place the oysters in the sandwich and fold the top of the roll over.

dungeness crab & shrimp melt

*We take you back to your childhood with this one.
Maybe back then the topping was tuna salad. We've dressed
it up a little. Either way, an English muffin, a great
seafood salad and melted cheese is as comforting a
combination today as it was in our younger years.*

Yield: 2 sandwiches

2 English muffins
5 ounces crab meat
5 ounces bay shrimp
2 tablespoons minced onion
2 tablespoons minced celery
1/2 cup mayonnaise
Pinch of salt

Pinch of pepper
1 teaspoon freshly squeezed
  lemon juice
4 (1/4-inch thick) slices tomato
2 tablespoons herb vinaigrette
4 slices mild or medium
  cheddar cheese

Split the English muffins and toast them. Combine the crab meat, shrimp, onion, celery, mayonnaise, salt, pepper, and lemon juice to make a crab and shrimp salad. Spoon 1/2 of the salad on each muffin half. Dip the tomato slices in your favorite vinaigrette dressing and allow the excess to drain off. Place the coated tomato slices on the sandwiches, and top with cheese slices. Place under the broiler to melt the cheese.

Chef's note: The crab salad will not be hot. If you want the sandwiches to be hot all the way through, place them under the broiler without the cheese for 2 to 3 minutes and remove. Add the cheese and place back under the broiler until the cheese melts. Serve hot.

spenger's fish tacos

Fish tacos have been a favorite Southern California street-vendor food for many years. They make a great snack or light meal. Almost any fish may be used, so pick your favorite and enjoy.

Yield: 6 tacos

1/4 cup Chili Marinade (see below)

12 ounces any firm fish, diced to about 1 inch

3 tablespoons canola oil

6 (6-inch) flour tortillas

1 avocado, cut into 12 slices

2 cups finely shredded cabbage

3/4 cup shredded Monterey Jack cheese

3/4 cup shredded cheddar cheese

6 tablespoons mayonnaise

1 tablespoon chipotle pepper purée

3 ounces sour cream

Marinate the fish in the Chili Marinade (see recipe below) for five minutes. In a large, nonstick pan, sauté the fish in canola oil. Cook the fish until almost done, about 2 minutes. Set aside. Wrap the tortillas in a damp towel or place them in a plastic bag, then warm them in a microwave for 20 to 30 seconds. Place the tortillas on the counter. Combine the mayonnaise and the chipotle, and spread the mixture on the tortillas. Layer the remaining ingredients and the fish onto the tortilla. Gently fold the tortilla in half.

Chili Marinade:
1/2 cup vegetable oil
1 tablespoon chipotle pepper purée
1/2 tablespoon each: chili powder, cumin, and paprika
2 tablespoons chopped fresh cilantro
1 tablespoon honey

Mix together.

salmon clubhouse sandwich

A classic sandwich done "fish-house style."
Grill the salmon just before building the sandwich.

Yield: 1 sandwich

1 (5-ounce) salmon fillet
3 slices sourdough bread
2 pieces iceberg lettuce, cut to fit the bread
3 (1/8-inch thick) tomato slices
Dash of salt and pepper, for seasoning salmon
3 slices cooked bacon, warm and crisp
3 tablespoons mayonnaise

Cut the salmon to fit the bread. Two pieces work best. Season the salmon with salt and pepper. Grill. Toast the bread and spread 1 tablespoon of mayonnaise on each slice. Place the lettuce and the salmon on one slice of bread. Place a second slice of bread on top, then place the lettuce, tomato and bacon on top of it. Place third slice of bread on top. Secure the sandwich with 4 toothpicks or skewers. Arrange on a plate with the cut side facing out.

new england lobster roll

If you've ever been in New England, you're probably familiar with these fabulous sandwiches. Lobster shacks and beachside restaurants throughout the region have made them everyone's favorite. The key is the bun type of hot dog roll that is split on the top and has no crust on the sides. We offer suggestions and substitutions for these buns if you can't find them.

Yield: 4 sandwiches

1 1/2 pounds lobster meat
3 tablespoons minced onion
3 tablespoons minced celery
1 teaspoon freshly squeezed lemon juice
1 cup mayonnaise
3/4 teaspoon salt
3/4 teaspoon pepper
4 oversized hot dog buns
1 tablespoon softened or melted butter
Lemon wedges for garnish

Fold the lobster meat, onion, and celery into the mayonnaise. Season with lemon, salt, and pepper. Coat the bun with the butter on the surfaces that have no crust. Toast the buttered surfaces as you would for a grilled-cheese sandwich. Fill the toasted bun with the lobster mixture. Serve with cole slaw and lemon wedges.

About the buns: We suggest that you use the largest hot dog buns you can find. Turn them sideways, so the split side is up. Shave a little of the crust off the top and bottom of the bun. Optionally, you can buy sub or Hoagie rolls, shave the side crust and split them on the top. This is just a little bit of work, but it's well worth the effort, because only grilled rolls make the sandwiches authentic... and delicious!

seafood fettuccini alfredo

This is the number one most popular pasta dish throughout our restaurants. Creamy, rich, full of great seafood—this is a winner for any occasion! The bonus is in the simplicity of its preparation. We use dry pasta in our restaurants, but feel free to use fresh pasta if you prefer.

Yield: 2 servings

1/2 pound dry fettuccine
2 tablespoons butter
2 tablespoons chopped garlic
6 ounces small shrimp (70/90 per pound), peeled and deveined
6 ounces bay scallops
1/8 teaspoon salt
1/8 teaspoon pepper
8 ounces heavy cream
1/2 cup grated Parmesan cheese
1 teaspoon chopped fresh parsley

Boil the fettuccini to the al dente stage. Drain very well. Lightly sauté garlic in butter. Add shrimp and scallops. Cook for 1 minute. Add cream, salt, pepper, and Parmesan cheese. Cook and stir until reduced to a light cream sauce. Add the cooked fettuccine to the seafood mixture, and toss well. Pour into a large pasta bowl, and sprinkle with chopped parsley.

salmon penne
WITH wild
mushrooms

Salmon, wild mushrooms, and hazelnuts are the essence of the Pacific Northwest. If you can't find wild mushrooms, domestic button mushrooms or shitakes will work just fine. Like all of our pasta dishes, this comes together quickly for a weeknight dinner.

Yield: 2 servings

1/2 pound dry penne pasta
12 ounces salmon, diced to about 1/2 inch
Flour, to dust
3 tablespoons butter
1 tablespoon chopped garlic
1 tablespoon chopped shallots
1/2 cup sliced wild mushrooms
1/4 cup white wine
3/4 cup heavy cream
1/4 teaspoon salt
1/4 teaspoon pepper
3 tablespoons chopped, toasted hazelnuts
1 tablespoon chopped fresh parsley

Boil the pasta to the al dente stage. Drain well. Dust the salmon in flour. Sauté in butter for 1 minute. Add the garlic, shallots, mushrooms, and salt and pepper. Cook until garlic is golden and mushrooms are tender. Deglaze with white wine. Reduce by half. Add cream and reduce to a medium consistency. Place in a pasta bowl. Pour the salmon over pasta. Sprinkle hazelnuts and parsley on top and serve.

salmon penne
WITH pesto cream sauce

Here's a nice pasta for spring or summer when the wild salmon are running. It may be a bit rich, but the pesto cuts through, balancing the flavors.

Yield: 2 servings

1/2 pound dry penne pasta
3 tablespoons butter
10 ounces salmon, cut into 1-inch pieces
2 tablespoons minced shallots
1 tablespoon minced garlic
1/8 teaspoon salt
1/8 teaspoon pepper
1/2 cup fresh asparagus tips, trimmed into 1-inch pieces
10 artichoke heart quarters
3/4 cup heavy cream
3 tablespoons prepared pesto
1/4 cup Parmesan cheese
2 teaspoons chopped fresh parsley

Boil the pasta to the al dente stage. Drain well. Sauté salmon in butter for 1 minute. Add shallots, garlic, asparagus tips, artichokes, and salt and pepper. Cook until garlic is golden and asparagus is tender. Add cream and pesto. Reduce to a medium consistency. Drain pasta well and add to salmon mixture. Toss. Place in large pasta bowl. Sprinkle with Parmesan cheese and chopped parsley.

spicy shrimp linguini

If you like your pasta spicy, then this one's for you.
If you prefer, you can certainly "tame" the spice by using
fewer crushed red chiles, but if you really like it hot...
We make our own roasted tomato sauce, but you can
certainly make life easy by picking up your favorite
tomato sauce at the grocery store.

Yield: 2 servings

1/2 pound dry linguini
3 tablespoons olive oil
12 to 14 medium shrimp, peeled and deveined
2 tablespoons minced garlic
1/2 cup sundried tomatoes, julienne cut
2 teaspoons crushed red pepper
1/8 teaspoon salt
1/8 teaspoon pepper
4 tablespoons butter
1 1/2 cups Roasted Tomato Sauce (page 180)
2 tablespoons chopped fresh basil
1 tablespoon chopped fresh parsley
3 tablespoons grated Parmesan cheese

Boil the linguini to the al dente stage. Drain well. Sauté shrimp in oil for 1 minute.

Add sundried tomatoes, garlic, red pepper, salt, and pepper. Add butter, tomato sauce, drained pasta, and basil. Toss well. Serve in a large pasta bowl. Garnish with chopped parsley.

tortelloni WITH crab & gorgonzola

We created this dish at Jake's Famous Crawfish Restaurant in Portland, Oregon, because we love the sharp Gorgonzola that flavors the sauce. As with most of our pasta recipes, it's best if you precook the tortelloni then roll them into the sauce when you're ready to serve. This technique gives you more control over the dish as you can concentrate on the seafood and sauce at serving time.

Yield: 2 servings

1/2 pound dry or 1 pound fresh tortelloni, cheese filled, precooked, rinsed, and drained
8 ounces Dungeness crab meat
6 ounces Gorgonzola cheese
2 tablespoons butter

2 teaspoons minced shallots
1/4 cup dry white wine
1/2 cup cream
Salt and pepper
1 tablespoon chopped fresh parsley

Pick over the crab meat to remove any lingering shell fragments. Set aside 1/3 of the crab for a garnish. Crumble the cheese. Sauté the shallots in butter over low heat until softened. Add wine and cream and heat to a boil. Add crumbled cheese and the rest of the crab. Reduce the sauce over high heat for 1 minute. Add the tortelloni and continue cooking over high heat for another 2 minutes. Season with salt and pepper and transfer to dinner plates. Garnish the tortelloni with reserved crab and sprinkle with chopped parsley.

manila clams in wine sauce WITH linguini

This is one of the all-time classics of Italian cuisine in America. The addition of fresh clams makes such a difference and adds to the visual appeal.

Yield: 2 servings

1/2 pound dry linguini
4 ounces olive oil
4 tablespoons minced garlic
4 tablespoons minced shallots
2 cups white wine
20 Manila clams
8 ounces chopped clams, fresh or canned
1 cup cream
1 teaspoon salt
1 teaspoon pepper
4 tablespoons butter
4 tablespoons grated Parmesan cheese
4 teaspoons chopped fresh parsley

Boil linguini to the al dente stage. Drain well. Sauté the garlic and shallots in olive oil over medium heat. Add the wine and bring to a boil. Add the whole clams and steam until they begin to open. Add the chopped clams, cream, salt, and pepper. Cover the pan until the clams are completely opened. Stir in the butter. Pull pasta out and place into bowls. Top with the clams in sauce. Arrange the clams on top. Sprinkle with grated Parmesan cheese and parsley.

fettuccini alfredo WITH **boursin & grilled shrimp**

Boursin cheese, available in most grocery stores, adds a tangy and herbal backdrop to a traditional Alfredo sauce and complements the smoky grilled shrimp perfectly. Skewered shrimp are easier to handle on a grill, so you can leave them on the skewers, or remove them to serve.

Yield: 2 servings

1/2 pound dry fettuccini
1/2 cup vinaigrette dressing
20 medium shrimp, peeled and deveined
2 tablespoons chopped garlic
1 tablespoon butter
6 ounces reduced cream
4 ounces Boursin cheese
3 tablespoons grated Parmesan cheese
1 tablespoon Parmesan cheese and parsley, mixed

Boil the fettuccini to the al dente stage. Drain well. Marinate the shrimp in the vinaigrette for an hour or two. Remove the shrimp from the marinade and skewer. Grill the shrimp. Remove them from the skewers and set aside. Sauté the garlic in butter. Add the cream and Boursin. Simmer for 1 minute. Add the pasta and Parmesan to the pan. Toss. Pour the pasta into a bowl and mound the shrimp on top. Scatter the Parmesan-parsley mix on top.

scampi-style shrimp & roasted tomato linguini

This dish combines classic shrimp sautéed in garlic with linguini tossed in our deeply flavored Roasted Tomato Sauce. The result is full of flavor and is a garlic lover's delight. We use the largest shrimp generally available in this country (11 to 12 per pound). If you use smaller shrimp, remember to serve more of them.

Yield: 2 servings

1/2 pound dry linguini
3 tablespoons olive oil
10 large shrimp (the biggest you can find), peeled and deveined
3 tablespoons chopped garlic
1/4 cup white wine
2 cups Roasted Tomato Sauce (page 180)

1/2 teaspoon crushed red pepper
3 tablespoons heavy cream
3 tablespoons chopped fresh basil
1 teaspoon kosher salt
2 tablespoons butter
2 teaspoons chopped fresh parsley

Boil pasta to the al dente stage. Drain well. Heat oil to the smoking point. Add the shrimp and allow them to brown on one side for 30 seconds. Turn the shrimp and add the garlic to sauté. Deglaze with the white wine for 15 to 20 seconds. Add the Roasted Tomato Sauce and crushed red pepper. Toss. Add cream and basil. Toss again. Season with salt and toss in the butter. Move the shrimp to a plate and set aside. Toss the pasta in the pan, then pour the pasta into your serving bowls. Top the pasta with the shrimp and garnish with chopped parsley.

seafood

classics

Our company's culinary heritage is rooted in the traditions of "old-school" fish-house restaurants. We've been paying tribute to the great seafood dishes of that heritage since we opened our first restaurant in 1972. Since then, we have fried hundreds of thousands of crab cakes, grilled tons of fresh swordfish and too many shrimp to keep track of, and used the comfort and simplicity of these and other classics as the foundation for our menus. Now you can reproduce these dishes to preserve the old fish-house heritage right in your own home.

lobster pot pie

From down home to Down East, everyone loves pot pie. Replace the more typical chicken or turkey with the great American lobster, and you have something extraordinary.

Yield: serves 6

1 cup diced onion (large dice)
1 cup peeled and diced carrots
1 cup diced celery (large dice)
3 ounces clarified butter
1/2 cup flour
2 cups chicken or fish stock
1 1/2 cups heavy cream
1/4 cup sherry

1/2 teaspoon dried thyme
1/2 teaspoon Old Bay Seasoning
1 1/2 pounds cooked lobster meat
1/2 cup frozen peas
1 pie dough (page 179), rolled out to completely cover a 9 by 12-inch baking pan

Preheat over to 400°F. Sauté the onions, carrots and celery in butter until slightly soft. Add the flour. Blend well and cook for 2 to 3 minutes. Add the stock, cream, and sherry, and whisk until smooth. Season and add the lobster and peas, and simmer for 3 to 4 minutes. Pour the mixture into a 9 by 12-inch baking dish. Carefully place the pie dough over the mixture without stretching the dough, and seal the edges as you would for any other pie. Bake for 30 minutes, or until the crust is nicely browned.

boston baked cod

Simple is best when it comes to cooking a great seafood dish.
Cod from the East Coast are as simple as they come.
So is this classic from the New England region.

Yield: 2 servings

2 (6-ounce) cod fillets
4 tablespoons dry, white wine
2 ounces water
1 teaspoon salt
1 teaspoon pepper
2 ounces Lemon Butter Sauce (see beurre blanc sauce page 173)

Blend the following:
1/4 cup Panko bread crumbs
3 tablespoons melted butter
2 tablespoons chopped fresh parsley
Pinch of salt
Pinch of pepper

Preheat the oven to 400°F. Place the cod in a baking dish and pour the wine and water over the top to moisten the fish. Season with salt and pepper, and top with breadcrumbs. Roast the fillets until golden brown, about 7 to 8 minutes. Place the cod on a serving plate and drizzle with the Lemon Butter Sauce. Garnish with parsley.

crab imperial

It doesn't get more traditional or classic than this Chesapeake mainstay. Diners along the Eastern seaboard have been reveling in Crab Imperial for generations.

Yield: 4 servings

4 tablespoons butter
1/4 cup finely diced red and green bell peppers
1/4 cup finely diced onions
3/4 cup mayonnaise
1 tablespoon Dijon mustard
1 tablespoon Worcestershire sauce
1/4 teaspoon Tabasco sauce
1/2 teaspoon freshly ground pepper
1 teaspoon Old Bay Seasoning
1 1/2 pounds Lump crab meat
1 beaten egg
1/4 cup mayonnaise

Preheat the oven to 400°F. Sauté the peppers and onion in butter to soften. Cool before mixing. Combine the 3/4 cup of mayonnaise, Dijon mustard, Worcestershire sauce, Tabasco sauce, pepper and Old Bay Seasoning with the cooled vegetables. Blend. Add the crab meat and fold carefully to mix, being careful not to break up the crab. Divide the mixture into 4 individual oven dishes or casseroles. Bake for 15 to 20 minutes. Increase oven temperature to broil. Blend the egg and the remaining mayonnaise and spoon over each Imperial. Broil the imperials for a minute until brown.

seafood macaroni & cheese

Macaroni and cheese is an American classic, usually associated with casual meals and kids. This version takes your childhood memories to new heights and makes this a recipe for special occasions as well as for family meals.

Yield: 4 servings

8 ounces quartered mushrooms
4 tablespoons butter
8 ounces small shrimp
8 ounces bay scallops
4 cups cooked elbow macaroni
1 1/2 cups Cheese Sauce (page 174)
Pinch of salt
Pinch of pepper
3 tablespoons chopped chives
4 tablespoons grated Parmesan cheese
4 tablespoons bread crumbs

Sauté the mushrooms in butter until lightly browned. Add the seafood and sauté for 1 to 2 minutes. Add the cooked macaroni and stir. Add the cheese sauce and blend thoroughly. Season with salt, pepper, and chives. Place the mixture in a casserole dish. Sprinkle with bread crumbs and the Parmesan cheese. Brown the scallops lightly under the broiler before serving.

jake's étouffée

*When Cajun cooking was just becoming mainstream
we were fortunate enough to get to know pioneer Chef
Paul Prudhomme, who was more than kind enough to
share his recipe for this classic stew from his kitchens.
Our version has been one of our most popular menu items
ever since. Use extreme caution with the hot roux!
It is fundamental to the success of the dish,
but it is very hot!*

Yield: 6 servings

1/2 cup diced onions
1/2 cup diced green bell pepper
1/2 cup diced celery
1/2 cup vegetable oil
3/4 cup flour
3 cups chicken or fish stock
3 tablespoons butter
3/4 pound small shrimp
3/4 pound diced, cooked chicken, light or dark meat
1/2 pound andouille sausage
1 bunch thinly sliced green onion, for garnish
6 cups cooked rice

Sauté the onions, peppers, and celery in a deep stock pot until lightly browned. Add the flour. Reduce heat and cook for 6 to 10 minutes over a low heat, stirring constantly to produce a dark roux. (The darker the better, but be very careful not to scorch the roux.) When the desired color is reached, carefully add the stock. Protect yourself from the splashing roux, as the mixture is very hot. Whisk the sauce until smooth and reduce heat to simmer. Heat the remaining butter in a separate pot and sauté the shrimp, chicken, and andouille for 3 to 4 minutes until fully cooked. Pour the meats into the sauce base and blend. Pour the étoufée into serving bowls and scatter with the sliced green onion. Serve with white rice.

razor clams

Mention razor clams to residents of the Pacific Northwest, and a sweet expression will come to their faces. This unique treat is prized for its rich, buttery flavor and the crisp, crunchy coating that this recipe creates. Cooking them quickly without crowding them in the pan is the key.

Yield: 2 servings

12 to 14 razor clams
Flour, to dust
2 whole eggs, beaten with a slight amount of water
2 cups Panko bread crumbs
3 ounces clarified butter (page 175)
4 ounces tartar sauce (page 181)

Pound the razors lightly with a tenderizing hammer to avoid toughness. Dip the razors in the flour first, then the egg, and finally in the Panko, pressing and coating completely. Heat the butter in a large sauté pan until just below the smoking point so as not to crowd the razors. Place the razors in the sauté pan evenly, so that they are not overcrowded, and sauté them quickly (no more than 2 minutes per side) until golden brown. *Do not over cook.* Serve with tartar sauce.

shellfish
pan roast

Pan Roasts were a mainstay in the original fish houses in New England at the turn of the twentieth century. They are really similar to stews, but tend to have less broth and more substance than a true stew. Whatever the recipe, they can be wonderful family meals or the focal point of a special occasion.

Yield: 2 servings

2 ounces vegetable oil
10 Manila clams
10 Black mussels
3 Dungeness crab legs
2 tablespoons chopped garlic
2 ounces onions, julienned
1/4 cup tri-colored peppers, julienned
6 medium shrimp, peeled to the tail
4 ounces red wine
4 ounces calamari, with tentacles
1 1/2 cups Roasted Tomato Sauce (page 180), or purchased
3/4 cup chicken or fish stock (or water)
1 tablespoon chopped fresh basil
1/2 teaspoon kosher salt
1/2 teaspoon crushed red chiles
1/2 teaspoon dried oregano

Heat the oil in a large sauté pan or brazier, and add the clams, mussels, and crab. Cover and cook for 1 to 2 minutes. Add the garlic, onions, peppers, and shrimp. Toss. Deglaze the pan with the red wine. Add the calamari, the Roasted Tomato Sauce, the stock, fresh basil, salt, chiles, and oregano. Toss. Finish, either in the oven or on the stove, until the shellfish are cooked and the shells are open. Pour the shellfish onto a serving plate and serve with garlic bread.

nantucket bay scallops

---

*For those lucky enough to live on the East Coast,
late fall and early winter is a wondrous time.
Autumn is the short but remarkably sweet season
for the Bay Scallops that are harvested off
Cape Cod and Nantucket Island. They are
the best scallops in the world. We are fortunate
to enjoy a great relationship with the
local harvesters, and Nantucket Bays are
proudly featured on our menus each season
throughout the region.*

Yield: 4 servings

1 1/2 pounds Nantucket Bay Scallops
4 ounces Lemon Butter Sauce (see beurre blanc sauce page 173)
3/4 cup seasoned breadcrumbs

Preheat the oven to 400°F. Place the scallops in an oven-proof serving dish, and spoon the Lemon Butter Sauce over them. Top with the breadcrumbs. Bake until the scallops are just barely cooked (6 to 7 minutes). Do not overcook, as these are best when they are slightly underdone.

seafood newburg

The "old-school" fish-house restaurants of the late nineteenth and early twentieth centuries provided many dishes for the current repertoire of American classics. Because those restaurants were the original inspiration for our menus, it's not surprising to see Seafood Newburg and other traditional fish-house dishes in our restaurants (and in our cookbooks) today.

Yield: 4 servings

2 ounces clarified butter (page 175)
1/4 cup finely diced onion
1 cup quartered mushrooms
8 ounces small shrimp, peeled
8 ounces Bay or Sea scallops
8 ounces cod, diced to about 1 inch
1 ounce sherry
4 ounces Newburg Sauce (page 177)
2 tablespoons chopped fresh parsley
Paprika, to dust

Place the clarified butter and the onions into a hot sauté pan and brown. Add the mushrooms and continue to sauté until they are lightly browned. Add the seafood and cook for 3 to 4 minutes. Deglaze with the sherry. Add the Newburg Sauce and simmer for 30 seconds. Pour into serving dishes or over rice. Sprinkle with the chopped parsley and paprika.

broiled
seafood platter

*Can't decide? Here's the solution restaurants have been
using for years. Create a classic combination platter featuring
a number of different fish and shellfish. This is an easy
way to provide something for everyone and create a
very impressive presentation.*

Yield: 4 servings

8 oysters
8 tablespoons Buttered Bread Crumbs (page 174)
4 (3-ounce) salmon fillets
12 large shrimp, peeled and butterflied
8 large sea scallops
4 (2-ounce) crab cakes (page 4 or 5)
8 ounces white wine
2 ounces melted butter
1 teaspoon salt
1 teaspoon pepper
2 ounces Lemon Butter Sauce (see beurre blanc sauce page 173)
2 ounces Northwest Berry Sauce (page 178)
1 tablespoon chopped chives

Preheat the oven to 400°F. Open the oysters, leaving them on the
half shell (page 20). Top each with a tablespoon of the Buttered
Bread Crumbs. Place the salmon, shrimp, scallops, oysters, and
crab cakes on a sheet pan or into a large baking dish. Brush with
butter and season with salt and pepper. Pour in the wine and bake
for 8 to 10 minutes. Place seafood on serving plates. Top the shrimp
and scallops with the Lemon Butter Sauce. Top the salmon with the
Northwest Berry Sauce. Sprinkle with chopped chives.

swordfish piccata

Simple and *quick. This is a classic way to prepare any number of meats and seafoods, from veal to chicken and beyond. Swordfish is a perfect match to the piccata preparation and makes an outstanding meal in just a few minutes.*

Yield: 2 servings

4 (3 to 4-ounce) swordfish medallions
1 ounce vegetable oil
1 ounce butter
Flour, to dust
1 tablespoon finely minced shallots
1/4 cup dry white wine
1 tablespoon capers
1 teaspoon freshly squeezed lemon juice
2 teaspoons finely shredded fresh sage
1 tablespoon cold butter
1 1/2 cups cooked rice

Place the swordfish medallions between two sheets of plastic wrap or waxed paper, and lightly pound them to 1/4-inch thickness. Heat the oil and butter together in a sauté pan. Dust the swordfish medallions in flour and sauté for 1 minute. Add the shallots for another minute, then remove them from the pan. Add the wine, capers, lemon juice, and the sage. Simmer for 1 to 2 minutes. Swirl in the butter. Place the medallions on the serving plates with the rice and pour the pan sauce over them.

halibut

We know that the typical family meal is not a multi-course event. Year after year, the fabulous wild halibut and salmon from the waters of the Pacific Northwest are popular choices of our guests. We felt these "kings of the sea" deserved their own section in this book to celebrate not only their popularity but also the quality and culinary heritage that they bring to our dishes. Still, there are many meals that do call for a first course. The recipes in this section will give you a variety of choices for when you wish to kick off your meal with style.

macadamia nut-crusted halibut

Halibut is a sweet and delicate fish to begin with; adding a crust of ground macadamia nuts really takes it over the top. The sauce is a tantalizing combination of richness and piquant flavors that are a match to this luxurious presentation.

Yield: 2 servings

2 (5 to 6-ounce) fresh halibut fillets
1 cup roasted, crushed macadamia nuts
1/2 cup Panko breadcrumbs
1 tablespoon freshly ground pepper
1/2 cup all-purpose flour
2 eggs
1/4 cup vegetable oil
1/2 cup Lemon Butter Sauce (see beurre blanc sauce page 173)
1/4 cup Major Grey's Chutney

Combine the nuts and breadcrumbs and blend well. Place on a large plate or in a pie pan. Season the flour with the salt and pepper, and place on a second plate or pan. Beat the eggs with a tablespoon of water or milk, and place in a third dish or pan. Arrange the 3 plates in a row in front of you, beginning with the seasoned flour, next, the eggs, and then the roasted Macadamias. First, dip the fillets in the flour, coating thoroughly and shaking off the excess. Next, dip the fish into the egg mixture, allowing the excess to drip off. Finally, roll the fillets in the nuts, pressing them in firmly to ensure that the fish is thoroughly coated. Pan-fry the fillets 3 to 4 minutes per side in oil over medium-high heat. Remove the fillets and allow them to drain briefly on paper towels. Place them on your serving dishes. Combine the butter sauce and the chutney, and pour over the halibut.

apple halibut

This dish is perfect for an autumn evening, when the halibut season is on and the apples have just been harvested. Select an apple with lots of juice and a tart flavor.

Yield: 2 servings

2 (6 to 7-ounce) fresh halibut fillets
Pinch of salt
Pinch of pepper
3 tablespoons flour
4 tablespoons vegetable oil
3 tablespoons butter
3 to 4 baby red potatoes, quartered and grilled
3 strips smoked, diced bacon
1/2 cup thinly sliced red onion
1 medium apple, peeled and thinly sliced
1/2 cup Lemon Butter Sauce (see beurre blanc sauce page 173)
2 tablespoons chopped chives

Season the halibut with salt and pepper. Lightly dust in the flour. Heat the oil in a sauté pan. Sear the halibut over medium-high heat until golden brown. Remove from the pan and hold in a warm oven. Sauté the bacon, red onion, and apples in the same pan for about 2 minutes. Place the red potatoes in the center of your plate. Pour the bacon, apples, and onions over the potatoes. Place the warm halibut on top. Pour the Lemon Butter Sauce over the fish, and sprinkle with chives.

cedar-planked salmon

This is the quintessential Pacific Northwest seafood preparation, dating back to the Native Americans who skewered chunks and sides of salmon with cedar to roast over an open fire. Here, we refine the process for indoor cooking. The wood can take any form as long as it is untreated and is "finished" on at least one side. You can buy roasting boards at many grocery stores or just go to your local hardware store and buy planks, siding or closet cedar.

Yield: 4 servings

1 cedar wood plank, finished on at least one side
1/4 cup vegetable oil
4 (6 to 7-ounce) salmon fillets
1/4 teaspoon salt
1/4 teaspoon pepper
1/2 cup Northwest Berry Sauce (page 178)

Preheat the oven to 400°F. Brush the sides of the cedar plank with oil. Place the salmon on the board, and moisten the fillets with a small amount of oil. Sprinkle with salt and pepper. Place the board in the hot oven and roast the fillets until done, 7 to 8 minutes. Salmon is perfectly cooked when it is still slightly pink in the center of the fillet. Drizzle the Northwest Berry Sauce on the side.

grilled coho WITH fennel, leeks, & chanterelles

Coho is a bit more delicate and finely textured than king salmon or sockeye, so it is best suited for this presentation, but you can substitute any species that is in season.

Yield: 2 servings

2 (6 to 7-ounce) coho fillets
2 tablespoons butter
5 to 6 sliced chanterelle mushrooms
1/2 cup sliced fennel
1/2 cup sliced leeks
1/2 cup white wine
1/2 cup chicken stock
1 cup heavy cream
Pinch of salt
Pinch of pepper
2 tablespoons vegetable oil

Sauté the chanterelles, fennel, and leeks in butter until soft and lightly browned. Add the wine, chicken stock, and cream. Reduce for 3 to 4 minutes. The sauce should be of medium thickness and have a rich ivory color. Season with the salt and pepper. Oil and grill the coho to desired doneness. Remove to a serving plate. Spoon the sauce over the fish, and serve.

grilled fillet OF
king salmon

Chinook is the traditional Native American name for the Pacific king salmon. Although red king salmon is by far the most prominent, white kings, usually from Alaska, are also available from time to time. Their ivory flesh and rich flavor make them highly sought after by knowledgeable Northwest diners.

Yield: 4 servings

4 (6 to 8-ounce) fillets of fresh king or chinook salmon, approximately 1-inch thick
Vegetable oil, to coat

Make sure that your fillets are free of bones and that the flesh is firm and intact.

Prepare the barbecue or preheat the range-top grill to medium-high heat. Make sure that the grill grates, and not just the fire itself, are hot.

Brush the grates with a little vegetable oil. The oil, along with the hot temperature of the grates, will prevent the fish from sticking and ensure proper grill markings on the salmon.

Coat the salmon lightly with vegetable oil and place on the grill so that the longest dimension of the fillet is at a 45-degree angle to the grill pattern.

If you like your salmon as we do, cooked medium to medium rare with a pink center, "mark" the fish by rotating it another 45 degrees after approximately 2 minutes. After 2 more minutes, flip the fillet over and grill on the other side for an additional 4 minutes. The salmon should be just barely cooked through, with a medium-pink center, and lightly charred with grill marks.

Prepared in this fashion, the salmon's naturally rich and distinctive flavor will be highlighted. However, there are a few acceptable variations:

- Serve accompanied by a beurre blanc sauce flavored with blackberry or orange (page 173).

- Rub the fillet with freshly squeezed lemon juice and chopped fresh dill prior to grilling.

- For a distinctively Northwest flavor, slow the fire down to medium-high and sprinkle dampened alderwood chips on your barbecue coals. Prepared in this manner, the salmon will take on a faintly smoky flavor reminiscent of the alder-smoked salmon prepared for centuries by Northwest Native Americans.

poached halibut IN mushroom broth

This is a beautiful, light presentation that lets the flavors of the ingredients shine through. It makes an elegant mid-summer dinner.

Yield: 2 servings

2 (5-ounce) fresh halibut fillets
Pinch of lemon-pepper
   seasoning
6 baby carrots
8 asparagus tips
6 plum cherry tomatoes, split
6 baby green beans
6 fingerling potatoes, halved

6 morel mushrooms (or any
   other mushroom)
1 cup Mushroom Consommé
   (recipe below)
5 drops truffle oil
Sprig of fresh cilantro, for
   garnish

Blanch the vegetables in advance until they are just barely cooked. Poach the halibut in the mushroom consommé to heat thoroughly. Place the vegetables in a serving bowl. Top with the poached halibut. Sprinkle the halibut with the lemon-pepper seasoning. Finish the dish with a few drops of truffle oil drizzled on the plate around the fish.

Mushroom Consommé:
2 ounces dried, wild mushrooms
1 celery stalk, chopped
1/2 carrot, chopped
1/2 onion, chopped
3 tablespoons olive oil
1 quart water

Simmer all ingredients and reduce to 1 1/2 cups. Strain through a fine-mesh strainer.

halibut & salmon medallions WITH potato-shrimp cakes

Salmon and halibut are arguably the two most popular fin-fish species in the United States. That certainly rings true in our restaurants. Here's a dish that avoids the challenge of deciding between the two for your meal. When you add the shrimp in the potato cake, you include the best of the shellfish world as well.

Yield: 2 servings

4 (2-ounce) halibut medallions
4 (2-ounce) salmon medallions
2 Potato-Shrimp Cakes (see recipe to the right)
4 roasted Roma tomato halves
3 tablespoons vegetable oil
2 tablespoons Lemon Butter Sauce (see beurre blanc sauce page 173)
1 teaspoon chopped fresh dill

Trim the medallions to make them about the same size and shape. Prepare the potato-shrimp mixture. Core and split the tomatoes lengthwise and roast in a low oven (250°F) for about 2 hours, or until they are somewhat dehydrated. Divide the potato-shrimp mixture into 2 cake-shaped portions and brown in oil for 4 to 5 minutes on each side. Meanwhile, melt the butter in another pan and sauté the fish medallions for about 2 to 3 minutes per side. Place the finished Potato-Shrimp Cakes in the center of your serving plates. Top each with 2 tomato halves. Arrange the medallions around the cakes. Drizzle the cakes and the fish with Lemon Butter Sauce. Sprinkle with dill.

Potato-Shrimp Cakes

Yield: 2 (6-ounce) cakes

1 pound potatoes, peeled and diced to about 3/4 inch
1/2 pound small shrimp, peeled and deveined
1 teaspoon salt
1 teaspoon pepper
1/4 cup cream
1/2 cup shredded medium cheddar cheese

Boil the potatoes in salted water until thoroughly cooked. It is better to overcook the potatoes a little bit than to undercook them. You want them to be slightly soft so they bind together. Sauté the shrimp briefly and combine with the drained potatoes. Let the mixture cool a bit, but not completely. The mixture should retain enough heat to slightly melt the cheese. Add the salt, pepper, cream, and cheese, and blend thoroughly. *Do not over-mix*. The mixture should bind together nicely. Form into cakes and chill. Brown in oil for 4–5 minutes on each side.

Pan-fry the fillets 3 to 4 minutes per side in oil over medium-high heat. Remove the fillets and allow them to drain briefly on paper towels. Place them on your serving dishes. Combine the butter sauce and the chutney, and pour over the halibut.

Variation: For Potato-Crab Cakes, substitute crab meat for the shrimp.

stuffed salmon
WITH **crab & shrimp**

While dining at McCormick & Schmick's in Portland, Oregon, Bill McCormick once called this dish "one of the most perfect meals I've ever had." For all its glory, it's really very easy to prepare—just a few ingredients blended together perfectly.

Yield: 4 servings

1 cup beurre blanc sauce (page 173)
4 (5-ounce) salmon fillets (not steaks)
6 ounces Dungeness crab meat
6 ounces bay shrimp
6 ounces brie, cut into 1/2-inch cubes
3 tablespoons mayonnaise
1 tablespoon chopped fresh dill
Pinch of salt
Pinch of pepper

Preheat oven to 400°F. Prepare the beurre blanc sauce and set aside. Split the salmon fillets lengthwise to form a pocket for the stuffing. Combine the crab, shrimp, brie, dill, salt, and pepper. Gently blend in the mayonnaise to bind the mixture. Divide the stuffing mixture between the four pocketed fillets. When full, let the flaps cover the stuffing so that only a small amount is exposed. Bake in a lightly buttered baking dish for 10 to 12 minutes. Transfer to dinner plates and spoon the beurre blanc over the fish.

sockeye salmon
WITH wild mushrooms

This recipe calls for sockeye salmon, but king, coho or Atlantic all work well. It also calls for wild mushrooms and cipollini onions, which can be difficult to find. These specialty items do make a difference, and elevate the dish to "very special." You can substitute button mushrooms and pearl onions with good results. Either way, the flavor of the fresh salmon will carry the meal.

Yield: 2 servings

3 cups chopped Swiss chard
4 tablespoons light olive oil
3 ounces fresh chanterelle mushrooms
3 ounces fresh morel mushrooms
8 roasted and skinned cipollini onions
4 tablespoons unsalted butter
2 (6 to 7-ounce) Sockeye salmon fillets
4 teaspoons chopped shallots
4 teaspoons chopped garlic
3/4 cup white wine
1/2 teaspoon salt
1/2 teaspoon pepper
3 tablespoons sundried tomato oil

Blanch the Swiss chard in boiling water until tender. Rinse in cold water. Sauté the chard in the olive oil and set aside. Sauté the mushrooms and onion in butter until tender and add to the Swiss chard. Season and grill (or bake) the sockeye. While the fish is cooking, return the mushrooms and chard to a hot sauté pan and add the shallots and garlic. Add the wine and reduce by half. Season with salt and pepper. Place the vegetable mixture in the center of each serving plate. Lay the fillets on the vegetables and drizzle a ring of sundried tomato oil around the fish.

sockeye salmon
WITH pesto-potato gnocchi

*This salmon preparation is absolutely filled with flavors.
The potato gnocchi are generally available in the frozen section
of better grocery stores. You could always pull out your
favorite Italian cookbook and make some from scratch.
We would applaud the effort, but it's not really necessary.*

Yield: 2 servings

2 (6 to 7-ounce) sockeye salmon fillets
2 tablespoons minced garlic
2 tablespoons minced shallots
8 tablespoons olive oil
1/8 cup sliced mushrooms
4 tablespoons julienned sundried tomatoes
4 tablespoons julienned roasted red peppers
1 cup heavy cream
12 ounces potato gnocchi, cooked according to package directions
4 tablespoons prepared pesto
2 tablespoons grated Parmesan cheese
4 tablespoons toasted pine nuts
4 tablespoons balsamic reduction

Season and sear the fillets in a hot sauté pan. Place the fillets on an oven-proof plate and hold in a warm (150-200°F) oven. Return the sauté pan to the heat and add the olive oil, garlic, and shallots. Add the mushrooms, sundried tomatoes, and peppers. Add the heavy cream, gnocchi, pesto, and grated cheese. Cook to reduce enough cream to bind all of the ingredients. Spoon everything onto the center of a plate. Sprinkle with toasted pine nuts. Place the sockeye fillets on top of the gnocchi. Drizzle with balsamic reduction.

grilled halibut

Great ingredients kept simple is always a recipe for success. In this case, halibut from icy Alaskan waters presents the perfect foundation for this culinary philosophy. Use olive oil, balsamic vinegar, and fresh basil, and you'll have a very quick and simple preparation that's a winner every time.

Yield: 2 servings

2 (6 to 7-ounce) halibut fillets
Seafood seasoning or salt and pepper, to dust
2 tablespoons finely shredded fresh basil
2 tablespoons Extra virgin olive oil
1 tablespoon balsamic vinegar

Oil and season the halibut, and grill over a hot fire until just cooked. Transfer to serving plates, then scatter with the basil and drizzle with the olive oil and balsamic vinegar. Serve with grilled vegetables and your favorite potato or rice recipe.

southwest-bronzed halibut & prawns

Prepare this recipe on a sunny summer evening
and feel the warmth of the "Cuisine of the Sun."

Yield: 2 servings

2 (6-ounce) halibut fillets
4 large shrimp, peeled and deveined
Southwest seasoning, to coat
3 tablespoons vegetable oil
3 cups cooked rice
1/2 cup Tropical Fruit Salsa (page 178)
1/2 cup Avocado Salsa (page 173)
Fresh cilantro, for garnish

Dredge the halibut and shrimp in the Southwest seasoning. Heat the oil in a sauté pan and sear the seafood on both sides. The fish will take about 4 minutes per side. Cook the shrimp about 3 to 4 minutes total. Place the rice in the center of your serving plates. Place the halibut on top of the rice. Spoon the Avocado Salsa on the fish, followed by the shrimp and Tropical Fruit Salsa. Garnish with a sprig of cilantro.

pesto-crusted fillet of salmon

Pesto seems to be everyone's favorite sauce. When fresh basil is available and you can make it fresh, it truly is something special. We include a recipe for such times, but there are some very good "store-bought" pestos available if you don't have the time.

Yield: 1 serving

2 ounces Pesto-Bacon Mixture (page 179)
1 tablespoon Red Onion Relish (page 179)
1 (5-ounce) salmon fillet
1 ounce vegetable oil
3 ounces fresh spinach
1 teaspoon chopped garlic
2 tablespoons white wine
1 tablespoon cold butter
3/4 cup cooked rice

Prepare the Pesto-Bacon Mixture and the Red Onion Relish and set aside. Coat the salmon with the Pesto-Bacon Mixture in an even layer. Heat the oil in a Teflon sauté pan. Sear on medium-high heat, pesto-side down, for 3 to 4 minutes. Turn the fish over, add the garlic, spinach, and white wine to the pan, cover it and reduce the heat to low. Allow the fish to cook and the spinach to wilt for 3 to 4 additional minutes. Remove the fish and set aside. Place the spinach in the center of the serving plate and return the pan to the heat. Add the butter and swirl to melt. Place the salmon fillet on the spinach and top with Red Onion Relish. Drizzle the butter around the plate and serve with rice.

ies

Occasionally you need a special recipe to serve as the focal point of an important dining occasion in your home. This section offers several options. A couple may be a bit challenging and require extra time, organization, and culinary expertise. Others are special and surprisingly easy to prepare. Either way, these are the main-course dishes that will bring that extra level of "professional chef" style to your dining table.

corn-crusted snapper

The coating on this fish is fantastic and reflects the regional variety that we bring to our menus. This one comes from our restaurants in Texas, but it's a hit throughout the country. We like the Pacific snapper for this recipe, but rockfish, cod, Eastern snapper, or even a thick piece of sole or flounder will work as well. Serve this with your favorite rice dish and perhaps some black beans.

Yield: 2 servings

2 (5 to 6-ounce) Pacific snapper fillets
Pinch of salt
Pinch of pepper
Flour, to dust
1 cup Southwestern Corn Crust Batter (page 180)
1/4 cup canola oil
3 tablespoons butter
1 teaspoon Tabasco sauce
1 teaspoon chopped chives
1/4 cup pico de gallo or fresh salsa

Before cooking the fillets, ensure that they are free of bones. Season them with salt and pepper, and dust with the flour. Heat the oil until just below the boiling point. Dip the fish in the prepared Southwestern Corn Crust Batter, allow a little run off, then place the fillets in the hot oil. Cook until golden, 2 to 3 minutes per side.

While the fish is cooking, melt the butter and add the Tabasco and chives. Remove the fish from the oil, blot on paper towels, then place on the serving plates. Pour the seasoned melted butter over each fillet and top with 2 tablespoons of pico de gallo or fresh salsa.

lobster & bay shrimp crepes

Obviously lobster is a very "special occasion" item, with a matching price tag. But this recipe works wonderfully with shrimp or scallops or any combination of shellfish. It's a perfect brunch or lunch dish but—especially with the lobster filling—it really does make a unique and festive dinner.

Crepes can be purchased frozen and ready to thaw for use. Learning to make crepes from scratch takes a little practice, but they are relatively easy and fun once you get the hang of it.

Yield: 4 servings

1 pound lobster meat or other shellfish
Water or white wine
Freshly squeezed lemon juice
Pinch of salt
Pinch of pepper
2 cups quartered mushrooms
2 cups asparagus, cut into 1-inch pieces

3 tablespoons butter
1 1/2 cups heavy cream
1/4 teaspoon salt
1/4 teaspoon pepper
1 tablespoon chopped fresh dill
8 (6 to 7-inch diameter) crepes
8 to 10 tablespoons Dill Cream Sauce (page 176)

Poach the shellfish in simmering water, white wine, or a combination of both, seasoned with a squeeze of lemon juice, salt, and pepper. The shellfish should be just barely cooked. Remove the shellfish from the poaching liquid and set aside.

Lightly sauté the mushrooms and asparagus in the butter. Add the cream, and reduce to thicken. Season with the salt, pepper, and dill, and add the shellfish back in. Lay the crepes out on your working surface, and divide the mixture evenly between them, placing the mixture along the edge of the crepe that is closest to you. Roll up the crepes and place them in the center of your serving plates. Top each with a generous tablespoon of the Dill Cream Sauce.

sea scallop risotto

Rich in flavor and firmly textured, sea scallops are a delight to cook, and to eat. But they must be of the highest quality, never frozen or soaked, and as large as you can find. Taking the time to search for the best product will ensure a fabulous meal. During preparation, be careful not to overcook them, because even the finest sea scallops can be ruined if cooked beyond medium-rare to medium.

Yield: 2 servings

10 very large sea scallops
2 teaspoons seasoning salt
2 ounces vegetable oil
2 cups cooked risotto
1 1/2 cups chicken stock
1/2 cup green peas
2 tablespoons butter
1/4 cup finely grated fresh Parmesan cheese
6 stalks asparagus, cut into thirds and cooked
1/4 medium red bell pepper, finely julienned
1 1/2 cups Newburg Sauce (page 177)
2 tablespoons chopped fresh parsley, for garnish

Season the scallops with the seasoning salt and sear them in a sauté pan in very hot oil for 2 to 3 minutes per side. They should be just barely cooked, actually medium-rare. Heat the risotto with the chicken stock over moderate heat. Add the butter and peas and stir. Finish the risotto by stirring in the Parmesan cheese. Place the risotto in the middle of a large pasta bowl and pour the Newburg Sauce around the rice. Place the scallops on the sauce and around the risotto. Scatter the asparagus and red pepper juliennes on top of the risotto. Garnish with the chopped parsley.

balsamic dijon-braised sea bass

Sea bass is a wonderful, very versatile, fish. In this dish we complement very assertive flavors. If sea bass is not available, any number of other species can be used, from swordfish to tuna, to mahi mahi, to grouper. Like so many of the recipes in this book, this dish comes together quickly once the vegetables are diced—6 to 8 minutes in the pan and you've got dinner.

Yield: 2 servings

2 (6 to 7-ounce) sea bass fillets
Pinch of salt
Pinch of pepper
4 tablespoons olive oil
1 tablespoon minced garlic
2 tablespoons finely diced red
   bell peppers
2 tablespoons finely diced onion

2 tablespoons finely diced
   celery
2 tablespoons finely diced
   carrots
4 teaspoons Dijon mustard
1/4 cup white wine
1/4 cup Balsamic vinegar
1 tablespoon butter

Heat the olive oil in a large sauté pan. Season the fish with salt and pepper, and sear until golden brown. Add the garlic, red peppers, onion, celery, and carrots, and sauté for 2 to 3 minutes. Add the Dijon, white wine, and Balsamic vinegar to deglaze the pan. Turn the heat to medium or medium-low, and simmer for 3 to 4 minutes. Transfer the fish to the serving plates, swirl the butter into the pan to melt, and pour the vegetables over the fish. If you like, serve this preparation with rice or mashed potatoes.

monkfish &
mussels

Colorful, flavorful, and easy to prepare, this dish is a great choice for your guests. Once the Coconut-Curry Sauce is ready, the rest comes together in minutes. Monkfish is hard to come by in West Coast stores, and it is unique in having almost shellfish-like taste and texture. You can certainly substitute other large, firm fish fillets, although the finished dish will be different—it will still be very good.

Yield: 2 servings

1 ounce olive oil
1/4 teaspoon minced garlic
2 (6 to 7-ounce) monkfish fillets
1/2 cup shitaki mushrooms, julienned
1/2 cup sliced snap peas
1/4 cup red and yellow bell peppers, julienned
10 medium-sized black mussels
2 ounces white wine
3/4 cup Coconut-Curry Sauce (page 175)
2 tablespoons roughly chopped daikon sprouts, for garnish
1 1/2 cups cooked white rice

Heat the oil in a large sauté pan or skillet. Add the garlic and monkfish, and sauté lightly. Add the mushrooms, peas, and peppers, and sauté for one minute. Add the mussels and deglaze with white wine. Add the Coconut-Curry Sauce. Simmer for 4 to 5 minutes, or until the fish is done.

Place the rice on 2 large pasta or soup plates. Place the fish on the rice and lay the mussels evenly around the fish. Pour the sauce from the pan over the entire dish. Sprinkle with the daikon sprouts.

tuna au poivre WITH port demi-glace

Preparation of a true demi-glace, the base for the sauce in this recipe, is not a quick or simple process. We suggest saving time with purchased demi-glace powders or pastes, readily available in most stores. Using them makes this terrific tuna recipe a snap.

Yield: 2 servings

2 (6 to 7-ounce) yellowfin (ahi) or albacore tuna steaks
Coarsely ground black pepper, to coat
4 ounces vegetable oil
1/2 cup thickly sliced yellow onion
12 ounces baby spinach, rinsed
1/4 cup port
2 teaspoons dried or fresh rosemary
2 teaspoons dried or fresh thyme
3/4 cup prepared demi-glace sauce
1 1/2 cups cooked white rice

Coat the tuna evenly with the black pepper. Sear the steaks in hot oil for 30 seconds on each side. Remove the tuna from the pan, add the onions and spinach, and sauté until the spinach is wilted, 2 to 3 minutes. Divide the vegetables onto 2 serving plates. Return the pan to the heat, add the port to deglaze, then add the herbs and the prepared demi-glace. Reduce the mixture for 1 to 2 minutes. *Tuna is best rare, but if you prefer to cook it through, continue cooking for another 2 to 3 minutes.*

Place the tuna steaks on the serving plates and strain the sauce over both the fish and the vegetables. Serve with the white rice.

pan-roasted corvina WITH potato-crab cakes

Corvina is a delicious member of the sea bass family. It can be hard to find outside of California and the Southwest. Like so many of our recipes, this preparation can be made with a number of other fish like mahi mahi, grouper, another sea bass, or even cod, all with terrific results. The combination of flavors and colors make this a very special meal.

Yield: 4 servings

4 (5 to 6-ounce) corvina fillets
Flour, to dust
1/2 teaspoon salt
1/2 teaspoon pepper
6 tablespoons vegetable oil
2 cups Corn Bisque (page 176)

4 Potato-Crab Cakes (page 89)
2 to 3 tablespoons Raspberry
   Balsamic Glaze (page 179)
3 tablespoons finely shredded fresh
   basil

Prepare the Corn Bisque, the Potato-Crab Cakes (a variation of the Potato-Shrimp Cakes on page 89), and the Balsamic Glaze, and set aside. Season the corvina with the salt and pepper. Dust the fillets with flour and pan-roast in oil over medium-high heat for 3 to 4 minutes per side. At the same time, fry the Potato-Crab Cakes until lightly browned on both sides. Optionally, you can bake the cakes in a very hot oven, but they will not be as brown or crisp.

Heat the Corn Bisque over low heat. Place the Potato-Crab Cakes on large pasta or soup plates. Place the corvina fillets on top of each cake.

Pour 1/2 cup of the bisque around each cake. Drizzle the Raspberry Balsamic Glaze over the surface of everything on the plate. Scatter the basil around, making sure some of it sits on top of the fillets.

pecan-crusted catfish

What a delightful combination: butter, freshly squeezed lime juice, and maple! Add some hot pepper flakes, and you have the perfect blend of salty, sweet, tart, and spicy.
Catfish has become one of the most popular items on our menus—not just in the South as some might think— but throughout the country. It's very mild, but firm, and well-suited to a variety of preparation styles.
As a bonus, it is one of the most affordable fish on the market.

Yield: 2 servings

2 (6 to 7-ounce) catfish fillets
Pinch of salt
Pinch of pepper
Flour, to dust
2 eggs beaten with 1 tablespoon water
1 1/2 cups finely ground pecans
4 tablespoons vegetable oil
6 tablespoons butter
2 tablespoons freshly squeezed lime juice
2 tablespoons maple syrup
1/2 teaspoon crushed red chiles

Season the catfish with salt and pepper. Dust the fillets in the flour, then dip them in the egg mixture. Coat well with the ground pecans. Heat the oil in a large sauté pan or skillet, and pan-fry the fish on both sides until nicely browned, 3 to 4 minutes. While the fish is cooking, combine the butter, the lime juice, maple syrup, and crushed red chiles, and heat just to melt the butter, not to sizzling hot. Place the cooked fillets on serving plates and pour the butter mixture over the fish.

tuna takashimi

This dish can be very dramatic, even spectacular. There are many steps for making such a magnificent impression. Think of this one as "extra credit" for when you have the time and the desire for a challenge. None of the elements is difficult, but each will take time and organization. This recipe will give you a true sense of the complexity—and fabulous results—that go along with following some of the finest restaurant recipes.

Yield: 4 servings

1 quart vegetable oil for deep frying
4 (5-ounce) ahi tuna "log cuts"
Cajun or Blackening spice, to dust
3 tablespoons vegetable oil
4 (6-inch) egg roll skins, fried like a taco shell
2 cups wasabi mashed potatoes (page 113)
4 ounces wasabi buerre blanc (page 113)
1 cup Asian Slaw (page 112)
4 teaspoons wasabi paste
soy reduction, for garnish
Chili oil (page 112), for garnish
Chive oil (page 113), for garnish
Black and white sesame seeds, for garnish
2 to 3 tablespoons pickled ginger

Pour the quart of vegetable oil in a medium-sized sauce pan and heat to 360°F (or, until a small piece of egg roll skin bubbles and fries when dropped into the hot oil). Add the egg roll skins one at a time and fry until crisp. If you have a small strainer that will fit into the pot, lay the egg roll skins in it to help them hold their shape (you want them to be bowl-shaped).

Heat the 3 tablespoons of vegetable oil in a sauté pan until smoking hot. Meanwhile, coat the ahi "logs" lightly in the Cajun spice and sear them for 10 seconds on each side. (Cook longer if you need your tuna

(continued on the next 2 pages)

111

to be fully cooked. For this dish, it is meant to be very rare.) Set the tuna aside and allow it to cool to room temperature.

Prepare the wasabi mashed potatoes and the buerre blanc sauce, and then gather the remaining ingredients together before assembling the dish. Slice each ahi log into 5 to 8 thin slices. Place the egg roll "bowls" on each plate and put 1/2 cup of potatoes into each one. Lay the ahi slices and the potatoes across the egg roll shell in a spiral row from top to bottom, as shown. Place 1/4 cup of the Asian Slaw at the bottom of the row of ahi, and drizzle the buerre blanc sauce over everything. Drizzle the soy reduction and the oils in a circular pattern around the plate. Scatter with the sesame seeds. Place the pickled ginger and wasabi paste on the plate for dipping.

Asian Slaw:
1 cup thinly sliced bok choy
1 cup thinly sliced nappa cabbage
1 cup red bell pepper, julienned
1/4 cup chopped fresh cilantro
1/4 cup green onions, cut on bias

For the dressing:
1 1/2 teaspoons finely diced ginger
3 tablespoons soy sauce
2 teaspoons sesame oil
1 teaspoon brown sugar

Mix the bok choy, cabbage, red pepper, cilantro, and onions together. Mix the ginger, soy sauce, sesame oil, and brown sugar in a separate bowl. Mixing may be done a day in advance. Dress the Asian slaw twenty minutes before serving the Takashimi, tossing it to evenly distribute the dressing.

Chili Oil:
1/2 cup vegetable oil
1 tablespoon chili powder

Blend the oil and chili powder in a blender for 5 minutes, then strain the mixture through a coffee filter. Place the finished oil into a squirt bottle and set aside. This oil may be made a day ahead of time.

Chive Oil:
2 bunches fresh chives
1/2 cup vegetable oil

Blend the chives and vegetable oil in a blender for 5 minutes. Place the finished oil into a squirt bottle and set aside. This oil may be made a day ahead of time.

Soy Reduction:
3/4 cup soy sauce
1 1/2 tablespoons brown sugar
1 tablespoon cornstarch
2 tablespoons water

Place the soy and brown sugar into a pot and boil. Mix the cornstarch and water. When the soy comes to a boil, add the cornstarch, then whisk and remove from heat. Let the mixture cool and place it into a squirt bottle. This sauce may be made a day ahead of time. Refrigerate.

Wasabi Mashed Potatoes:
3 cups cooked and mashed russet potatoes
3 tablespoons wasabi powder
1/4 cup heavy cream
4 tablespoons butter
1/2 teaspoon salt

Combine the cream and wasabi powder and blend well. Mix into the mashed potatoes. Add the butter and salt to taste.

Wasabi Beurre Blanc:
1 finely chopped shallot
4 ounces white wine
6 ounces butter
wasabi powder to taste

Combine the white wine and shallot in a sauce pan and reduce to 3 tablespoons. Remove the pan from heat and whisk in the butter. Strain and add the wasabi powder to taste.

cashew-crusted tilapia

Here's a recipe for one of the top-selling items on our menus for many years. Inspired by the flavors of the Caribbean, the sauce, seasoned with vanilla, lime, saffron, and hot habanero peppers, is what makes it special. We like to use tilapia for the fish, as it is readily available and works well with the flavors of the preparation. Mahi mahi, grouper, or sea bass are excellent substitutes.

Yield: 2 servings

2 (5 to 6-ounce) tilapia fillets
Flour, to dust
2 eggs, beaten with 2 tablespoons milk
1 1/2 cups finely ground cashews
1/4 cup vegetable oil
1/2 cup Jamaican Rum Butter
  Sauce (page 177)

1 tablespoon finely minced red
  bell pepper
1 tablespoon finely minced
  yellow bell pepper
1 tablespoon finely minced
  green bell pepper
2 tablespoons scallions, sliced
  to about 1/4 inch

Bread the fillets by first dusting them with the flour, then dipping them in the beaten egg mixture, and finally coating them thoroughly with the ground cashews. It is best to do the breading an hour ahead of serving time, then allow the fish to rest in the refrigerator before cooking. While the fish is resting, make the Jamaican Butter Sauce and keep on the stove, but not over direct heat. (The sauce will break down if it is too hot.)

Heat the oil in a large sauté pan or skillet and pan-fry the tilapia. Cook the fish on both sides until golden brown, 2 1/2 to 3 minutes per side. Place the fish on serving plates and pour the sauce over them. Combine the peppers to make a "pepper confetti," and sprinkle the dish with the scallions and peppers.

This dish is best when accompanied by rice and a simple grilled, sautéed, or steamed green vegetable like asparagus, spinach, or green broccoli.

rockfish WITH sautéed bay scallops

Rockfish can refer to several different species. On the East Coast, especially in the Chesapeake area, Rockfish means wild striped bass. Any coastal flat fish or cod will be great for this dish, so enjoy what is indigenous to your area.

Yield: 2 servings

2 (6 to 7-ounce) rockfish fillets
Flour, to dust
2 ounces vegetable oil
Pinch of salt
Pinch of pepper
8 ounces bay scallops
2 ounces shallots, minced
4 tablespoons butter
2 ounces white wine
3 diced Roma tomatoes
2 tablespoons finely chopped fresh basil

Season the fish with the salt and pepper. Dust in the flour, and sauté over high heat, about 2 minutes per side. Remove the fillets to serving plates and keep warm in the oven while finishing the dish.

Pour off the cooking oil, return the sauté pan to high heat, and sauté the scallops and shallots in the butter for about 30 seconds. Add the remaining ingredients and continue cooking for just a minute more. Pour the scallops and sauce over the fish and serve with your favorite side dishes.

bronzed redfish
WITH shrimp creole sauce

Here's a recipe that is pure Gulf Coast in style. Redfish is one of the great coastal species around the country. They aren't always available, and almost never available outside the South, but, nonetheless, this is a great recipe to have in your collection. It can be substituted with snapper, rockfish, or even cod.

Yield: 2 portions

2 ounces olive oil
2 teaspoons chopped garlic
2 teaspoons chopped shallots
10 ounces small shrimp, peeled and deveined
2 ounces sherry
12 ounces Creole Sauce (page 176)
2 tablespoons cold butter
1 1/2 tablespoons Cajun or blackening spice
Vegetable oil, for cooking
2 (5 to 6-ounce) redfish fillets
1 1/2 cups cooked white rice

Sauté the shrimp, garlic, and shallots in the olive oil over high heat long enough to cook the shrimp and brown the garlic and shallots, 2 to 3 minutes. Deglaze the pan with the sherry then add the Creole Sauce and allow to heat. Add the butter and allow it to melt in, then set the shrimp aside while you prepare the redfish. Heat the vegetable oil until very hot, dust the fish with Cajun spice, and pan-fry or "bronze" it for 2 to 3 minutes on each side. Place the fillets on the serving plates and pour the shrimp sauce over the fish. Serve with the white rice.

lobster & shrimp enchilada

There are several elements to this preparation, but you can simplify the process by buying the cheeses shredded, mixed, or both, and the same goes for the enchilada sauce. Go to the store and pick your favorite. In fact, buy the shellfish already cooked, grab a package of tortillas, and suddenly this recipe is a breeze. Seafood enchiladas may sound a bit risky, but trust us, once you've tried them you'll wonder why you ever settled for plain-old ground beef and cheddar. A little hint for the tortillas: Heating them slightly before you begin will make them more pliable so they resist splitting during the cooking process.

Yield: 4 servings

8 (8-inch) corn tortillas
1/2 pound cooked lobster meat
1/2 pound cooked shrimp, peeled and deveined
3/4 cup shredded cheddar cheese
3/4 cup shredded pepper Jack cheese
1 1/2 cups Enchilada Sauce, purchased
1 1/2 cups shredded cheddar and pepper Jack cheese
2 cups Enchilada Sauce, purchased

Side Condiments:
1/3 cup to 1/2 cup Chipotle Aïoli (page 174)
1 cup Roasted Corn Salsa (page 179)

Preheat the oven to 375°F. Wrap the tortillas in a damp towel and heat them very slightly in the oven. Blend the lobster meat, shrimp, 1 1/2 cups of Enchilada Sauce, and cheeses to form the enchilada filling. Lay the tortillas flat on your working surface. Fill them with equal portions of the filling, roll them, and place them in a baking dish, seam side down. Coat the rolls with the remaining sauce, cover them with the cheese, and bake until the cheese is melted and bubbly.

Have the two condiment sauces available for those who want to add even more color and spice to these delicious enchiladas.

ealthy

As healthful eating becomes an ever-increasing concern for all of us, it is important that restaurants do their part towards providing choices and balance on their menus. This section is devoted to recipes that provide heart-healthy options, yet don't skimp on flavor. As a bonus, they are all very quick and easy to prepare.

♥ rainbow cobb salad

This entrée salad is all about color. *The variety of vegetables was selected to give you a beautiful presentation, and, as an added bonus, these deeply colored vegetables are rich in disease-fighting nutrients and antioxidants.*

Yield: 4 servings

1 1/2 cups cooked chicken or cooked (41 to 50 count) shrimp
1 1/2 cups medium diced red onion
1 1/2 cups medium diced carrot
1 1/2 cups medium diced cooked beets
1 1/2 cups blanched broccoli (small florets)
1 1/2 cups medium diced yellow bell pepper
8 cups shredded iceberg lettuce
1 cup shredded red cabbage
1 cup low-fat Ranch, blue cheese, or vinaigrette dressing
4 tablespoons freshly chopped parsley

Prepare the diced chicken or shrimp and vegetables (red onions, carrots, beets, broccoli, and bell pepper). Combine the lettuce and cabbage and toss with dressing. Divide the salad equally onto 4 plates or bowls. Arrange 1/4 of the chicken or shrimp and 1/4 of each of the diced vegetables in decorative piles or rows on top of the lettuce mixture.

You may take some additional dressing and drizzle it over the salads. Sprinkle the tops with chopped parsley and serve.

♥ pesto-roasted salmon WITH spinach

Salmon is the most heart-healthy animal protein on earth. Here's a delicious way to add some extra flavor and color and still keep it low in calories, carbohydrates, and fat.

Yield: 4 servings

1 pound salmon fillcts
3/4 cup pesto (recipe below)
1 1/4 cups orzo pasta
1/2 of a 10-ounce (5 ounces), frozen, no-salt-added package of spinach

1/8 teaspoon ground nutmeg
1/4 cup shredded part-skim mozzarella cheese
Freshly ground black pepper
Lemon slices (optional)

Preheat the oven to 400°F. Cut the salmon into 4 portions and rinse. Set aside while you prepare the pesto. Lightly coat a baking dish with cooking spray.

Pat the fish dry with paper towels. Cut each salmon steak in half, removing as much of the bone, cartilage, and skin as possible. Coat the fillets in pesto and roast for approximately 8 minutes, or until the fish flakes.

Meanwhile, cook the orzo and spinach according to package directions. Drain the pasta well. Squeeze out the excess moisture from the spinach, then combine together with the pasta. Stir in the nutmeg, cheese, and pepper, and combine it with the pasta. Divide onto 4 plates. Place the salmon portions on top of the pasta.

Pesto
Ingredients:
1 cup fresh basil
1/4 cup freshly chopped garlic
1 cup chopped walnuts
1/4 cup Extra virgin olive oil
1/4 cup grated Parmesan cheese

Combine and blend thoroughly in a blender or food processor.

♥ northwest roasted halibut

The simplicity of the Northwest at its best... Beautiful fish and beautiful fruit, complementing one another perfectly.

Yield: 4 servings

4 (4 to 6-ounce) halibut fillets
2 tablespoons margarine, melted, but not hot
1 cup finely chopped hazelnuts
Vegetable oil spray
2 cups frozen, mixed berries (blackberries, raspberries, blueberries, and/or strawberries) thawed

Preheat the oven to 400°F.

Coat the halibut with the melted margarine and roll it in the crushed hazelnuts, coating well. Coat a baking pan with the vegetable spray and place the fish in the pan. Roast for 8 to 10 minutes or until the fish flakes.

While the fish is roasting, purée the berries in a blender or a food processor. Pass the purée through a strainer to remove the seeds. The sauce may be heated or not. Personally, I like the sauce unheated for contrast. It also has a "cleaner" flavor when unheated.

Note: Fresh berries do not work as well as frozen, as frozen berries produce a juicier sauce.

♥ crisp-roasted pork tenderloin

The marinade for this pork makes the dish. Chicken may also be substituted for the pork. Be careful not to overcook the pork tenderloins; because of their low-fat content, they can dry out easily.

Yield: 6 servings

3/4 cup finely chopped green onion, both white and green parts
1 cup poly-unsaturated oil, such as safflower or corn
1/2 cup freshly squeezed lime juice
4 teaspoons grated lime rind
2 tablespoons freshly grated ginger
2 tablespoons light soy sauce
1/2 teaspoon salt
1/2 teaspoon ground white pepper

2 small pork tenderloins
Vegetable oil spray
1 1/4 cups plain bread crumbs
2 tablespoons finely chopped fresh parsley
2 tablespoons finely chopped green onion
1 pound dry linguini, fettuccini, or spaghetti

Combine the onion, oil, lime juice and rind, ginger, soy sauce, salt, and pepper in a small bowl. Set aside.

Lay the pork tenderloin in a baking dish and pour 1/2 of the liquid mixture over all of the meat, turning to coat evenly. Cover the dish and refrigerate for several hours or overnight. Reserve the remaining mixture for the noodles.

Preheat the oven to 450°F. Lightly spray a baking dish with vegetable oil spray.

In a pie plate, combine the bread crumbs, parsley, and green onion. Stir to mix well and set aside.

Remove the tenderloins from the marinade and wipe off excess. Pat dry with a paper towel. Coat the meat with the crumb mixture. Place the pork in the prepared baking dish and roast approximately 30 minutes or until it reaches an internal temperature of 140°F.

While the pork is roasting, cook the pasta per package directions and toss with remaining marinade. Allow the pork to rest for a couple of minutes, then cut into 1/2-inch slices and lay over the noodles.

♥ seafood chili

Here's a heart-healthy spin on a classic American favorite. You won't believe how well seafood and white beans work to lighten the dish and provide great flavor.

Yield: 6 servings

1/2 pound dry white beans
2 cups low-sodium chicken broth (for use in cooking the beans)
1/4 cup olive oil
1 cup medium diced onions
1 cup medium diced celery
1/4 cup each: medium diced red, yellow, and green bell peppers
3 tablespoons chopped garlic
1 cup white wine
28 ounces canned, diced tomatoes with juice
1 tablespoon Tabasco sauce

4 tablespoons tomato paste
2 cups water or low-sodium chicken broth
1 teaspoon dried oregano
2 teaspoons chili powder
1 teaspoons cumin
2 tablespoons freshly chopped basil
2 tablespoons freshly chopped parsley
2 teaspoons dried thyme
1 pound seafood (cod, halibut, salmon, shrimp-or your favorite) diced into 1-inch pieces)

Soak the white beans in water overnight. Drain. Cook the beans in the chicken broth (enough to cover the beans) until tender, about 25 minutes.

Sauté the onions, celery, and peppers in the olive oil to soften. Add the garlic and cool for 1 minute. Add the wine and reduce for 1 to 2 minutes. Add the tomatoes and bring to a simmer.

Drain the cooked beans and add to the vegetable mixture along with the Tabasco, tomato paste, water or chicken broth, and herbs. Simmer for 10 to 12 minutes.

Add the seafood and simmer for another 3 to 4 minutes. Stir carefully to incorporate seafood without breaking it up too much.

♥ grilled tuna WITH mandarin orange & avocado salsa

This recipe is about perfectly grilled fish. Choose the best and freshest tuna you can find. The salsa is wonderfully fresh, full of flavor and color. It goes great with almost any grilled seafood.

Yield: 4 servings

Vegetable oil spray
1/2 cup chopped onion
1/2 teaspoon bottled, minced garlic
1 tablespoon balsamic vinegar or red wine vinegar
1 teaspoon firmly packed brown sugar
1/8 to 1/4 teaspoon crushed red pepper flakes
1 (15-ounce) can mandarin orange sections in light syrup, drained
1/3 cup chopped tomato
1/3 cup chopped avocado
1 tablespoon freshly squeezed lime juice
2 (8-ounce) tuna steaks

Spray a medium saucepan with vegetable oil. Place over medium-high heat. Add the onion and garlic, and cook until the onion is tender (about 5 minutes).

Stir in the vinegar, brown sugar, and pepper flakes. Cook and stir until the sugar dissolves (about 2 to 3 minutes).

Remove from heat and allow to cool slightly. Stir in the oranges, tomato, avocado, and lime juice. Set aside.

Spray the fish with vegetable oil. Place over medium-high heat on grill and cook for about 5 minutes per side. Slice each steak in half and divide into 4 portions. Serve fish topped with salsa.

♥ pan-roasted chicken breast

Roasting tomatoes, even in the middle of winter, brings out their sweetness and concentrates their flavor. Always use Roma tomatoes, as they are meatier. Add in the toasted pistachio nuts and you have great colors and textures to complement the chicken.

Yield: 4 servings

5 Roma tomatoes, sliced lengthwise (4 slices each)
Vegetable oil spray
1 teaspoon dried basil
1 teaspoon dried oregano
1 teaspoon dried thyme
1 teaspoon freshly ground black pepper
2 tablespoons olive oil
4 (4-ounce) boneless/skinless chicken breasts
1/2 cup sherry
1/2 cup low-sodium chicken stock
1/4 cup pistachios, shelled and toasted

Preheat the oven to 400°F.

Lay the sliced tomatoes on a baking pan that has been lined with foil and sprayed with vegetable oil spray. Combine the basil, oregano, thyme and pepper and sprinkle about 1/2 of the mixture over the tomatoes. Roast the tomatoes for about 1 1/2 hours or until lightly softened and caramelized, and remove.

Reduce the oven temperature to 350°F. Sprinkle remaining 1/2 of the herb mixture over both sides of the chicken breast.

Heat the olive oil in a sauté pan over medium-high heat. Sear the chicken in the pan until well browned. Then place the pan in the oven for 10 to 12 minutes.

Return the chicken to the stove top over high heat. Add the sherry and stock to the pan, and reduce to 1/2 cup.

Place the chicken breasts on 4 plates and pour *Jus* over each. Lay the tomato slices over the chicken and scatter with pistachios.

♥ fresh fruits & nuts for dessert

...with a little something extra

Simple, fresh and full of healthful benefits, this easy presentation celebrates the beauty of fresh fruit for dessert. The "little something extra" is an easy and fun addition that elevates the presentation.

Yield: 4 servings

Assorted fresh fruit (citrus, melon, apples, pears, peaches, bananas, pineapple, kiwi, berries, etc.) sliced
Whole, toasted hazelnuts, pecans, walnuts, and/or cashews
1 cup extra fruit, including berries, pineapple, and banana
1/2 cup plain yogurt
4 (4 to 6 ounce) sherry or cordial glasses

Arrange the sliced assorted fruit on 4 large serving plates in an attractive manner. Scatter with the toasted nuts.

Purée the extra fruit with the yogurt in a blender to make a smoothie. Pour into the 4 small glasses.

Add the fruit smoothies onto the serving plates as "a little something extra" along with the fruit and nuts.

seafood

grill

Many times the simplest, cleanest approach to cooking is best. This has never been more true than with seafood. A simply grilled, nicely charred piece of fish often needs nothing more than a little lemon butter or a sprinkle of fresh herbs to be delightful and tasty. This section offers a few ways to "gild the lily" when you want to add a bit more creativity to the grilling process.

grilled grouper
WITH asian
mustard sauce

*Grouper is a spectacular fish that lends itself to
bold flavors. This preparation is a great example.
The sauce is simultaneously bold, sweet, and hot.
Accompany it with steamed rice and a simple vegetable.*

Yield: 2 servings

2 (6 to 7-ounce) grouper fillets
Vegetable oil, to coat
1 teaspoon salt
1 teaspoon pepper
4 ounces Asian Mustard Sauce (below)
1/2 cup sliced scallions, for garnish

Coat the fish lightly with vegetable oil, season with the salt and
pepper, and grill over a hot fire. Spoon the mustard sauce over the
fish and garnish with the sliced scallions.

Asian Mustard Sauce:
1/2 cup Coeman's dry mustard
1/2 cup cider vinegar
2 large eggs
1/2 cup sugar

Combine the mustard and vinegar. Blend well, cover, and store
the mixture at room temperature for several hours or overnight.
Whisk the eggs to a froth, add the sugar, and blend to a paste.
Add the mustard mixture and cook the sauce over a double boiler
until it thickens to the consistency of hollandaise sauce.

grilled arctic
char WITH
pearl onions

Char is a cousin to salmon, but a bit milder and more finely textured. The pan-roasted vegetables in sage brown butter are a wonderful accompaniment and could be used with other fish or even chicken.

Yield: 2 portions

2 (6 to 7-ounce) Arctic char fillets
6 tablespoons olive oil
3 baby red potatoes, peeled and blanched
1 large portobello mushroom, diced
6 baby carrots, peeled and blanched
6 pearl onions, peeled and blanched
1 tablespoon finely shredded fresh sage
3 tablespoons cold butter

Grill the char over a hot fire and hold in a warm (180°F) oven while you sauté the vegetables. Heat a sauté pan, then add the olive oil. Sauté the pearl onions, portobello mushroom, potatoes and carrots until they're caramelized and cooked through. Pour off most of the oil, then add the sage and butter to the pan. Cook for an additional 1 to 2 minutes to brown the butter. It should have a nice golden brown color and a nutty aroma. Spoon the vegetables onto serving plates, remove the fish and place on top. Pour the butter over everything.

grilled mahi mahi WITH pan-roasted corn salsa

This is a great summer meal when local corn is plentiful, but it works well year-round. The flavors are decidedly southwestern, but the appeal is universal.

Yield: 2 servings

2 (6 to 7-ounce) mahi mahi fillets
4 ounces of your favorite barbecue sauce
4 ounces butter
1/2 cup finely diced onion
1/2 cup finely diced red bell pepper
1/2 cup finely diced green bell pepper
1 cup corn, fresh off the cob or frozen
2 teaspoons cumin
1 teaspoon salt
1 teaspoon pepper
2 teaspoons freshly squeezed lime juice
1/4 cup purchased salsa of your choice
4 cups black beans, cooked or canned

Grill the mahi mahi, basting frequently in barbecue sauce. Meanwhile, sauté the onions, peppers, and corn in the butter until cooked but still a bit crunchy. Season with the cumin, salt, pepper, and lime juice. Add the salsa. Toss to blend, and divide the mixture onto serving plates. Place a mound of the black beans in the center of each plate and top the beans with the mahi mahi fillets.

grilled prawns WITH tamarind glace

This is a fun and exotic preparation. There are several steps for this one, but the work is worth it. If you're not up for making your own Tamarind Glace, it's available at Asian groceries where you can also find the shrimp chips— which are like puffed rice when cooked.

Yield: 2 servings

4 metal or bamboo skewers
2 shrimp chips
1 cup vegetable oil
4 ounces Indonesian Fried Rice
  (see below)

1 ounce Tamarind Glace (page 181)
3 ounces Asian Cucumber Salad
  (page 173)
12 extra-large shrimp
4 wedges red onion

If using bamboo skewers, soak them in cold water several hours before use. Heat the oil in a small pan and fry the shrimp chips until they puff. Prepare the Indonesian Fried Rice, Tamarind Glace, and Asian Cucumber Salad, and set aside. Skewer the shrimp and the onion wedges, and grill for 2 to 3 minutes on each side over a hot fire. Stir-fry the rice. Place the skewers on the rice. Add the Asian Cucumber Salad on the side.

Indonesian Fried Rice:

1/2 cup long-grain or basmati rice
1/2 cup cooked, sliced snow peas
1 tablespoon chili paste

1 tablespoon sweet Thai chili
1 whole egg, scrambled

Cook the rice, then let it cool to room temperature. Stir-fry the rice in oil or a mixture of oil and butter, adding the remaining ingredients when the rice is hot. Stir well while the egg cooks into threads in the pan.

grilled rainbow trout

For this recipe we use a fabulously large, completely boneless trout that is raised by Clear Springs Farms. Its size is such that one fillet is the size of most whole trout available elsewhere. If you can find this fish, try it. There's no better trout on the market.

Yield: 2 servings

2 rainbow trout fillets
2 tablespoons vegetable oil
1/8 teaspoon salt
1/8 teaspoon pepper
2 tablespoons melted butter
1/2 teaspoon chopped chives
4 tablespoons Hazelnut-Apple Chutney (see below)

Coat the fish with vegetable oil, season with the salt and pepper, and grill over a hot fire. Transfer the fish to serving plates, coat each fillet with the melted butter, scatter with chopped chives, and top with 2 tablespoons of chutney. Serve with your favorite vegetable and potato or rice dishes.

Hazelnut-Apple Chutney:
1/4 cup diced onion
1 cup diced Granny Smith apples
2 tablespoons butter
2 tablespoons cider vinegar
1/2 cup Major Grey's Chutney

Sauté the onions and apples in the butter until they are soft and lightly browned. Add the vinegar. Stir together and remove from the heat to cool. When the apple mix has cooled to room temperature, combine it with the chutney and mix thoroughly.

grilled shrimp
WITH blackberry barbecue sauce

Blackberry Barbecue Sauce is outstanding on shellfish and chicken alike. It is rich, sweet, smoky, and a little spicy—all in one. It actually works best with frozen berries because they are often more concentrated than fresh ones.

Yield: 4 servings

24 shrimp, as large as available
12 strips bacon
4 metal or bamboo skewers
1 cup Blackberry Barbecue Sauce (page 173)

Cut each strip of bacon in half and wrap the pieces around each shrimp. Thread 6 shrimp on each skewer and, basting frequently with Blackberry Barbecue Sauce, grill the skewers over a hot fire until the bacon is cooked. The shrimp should be perfectly cooked at this point. Serve the grilled shrimp with your favorite accompaniments. We serve these shrimp with mashed sweet potatoes and sautéed greens for a very Southern dining experience.

grilled scallops
WITH sweet chili sauce

*For this or any other recipe using sea scallops,
the quality is everything. Never use frozen scallops.
And make sure the fresh scallops you buy haven't
been soaked. You want to find dry-packed scallops.
The difference is like night and day, and it will
ensure that your preparation is as delicious as
what we offer in our restaurants.*

Yield: 2 servings

1/2 cup sweet Thai chili sauce, purchased
1 tablespoon chili paste with garlic
1 tablespoon chopped fresh cilantro
1 tablespoon rice wine vinegar
10 very large sea scallops
2 teaspoons black and/or white sesame seeds, for garnish
2 cups stir-fried vegetables
2 cups cooked white rice

Combine the chili sauce, chili paste, cilantro, and vinegar, and
blend thoroughly. Grill the scallops, using 1/2 of the chili sauce as
a baste, until just barely cooked through. The scallops should be
medium-rare. Place 1/2 of the stir-fried vegetables in the center
of 2 serving plates. Place a mound of the white rice on top of the
vegetables. Spoon 2 ounces of the remaining sauce around the
outside of the plate. Place scallops evenly around the plate on the
sauce. Garnish with sesame seeds.

grilled swordfish

There is nothing quite like a thick swordfish steak grilled over an open flame, a little bit charred, and yet moist and juicy. Top it with a flavorful compound butter like the one in the recipe below, and you have a "center of the plate" entrée that's a winner for any occasion.

Yield: 2 portions

2 (7 to 9-ounce) swordfish steaks
2 tablespoons vegetable oil
1/4 teaspoon salt
1/4 teaspoon pepper
2 1/2-inch slice of Sun-dried Tomato Butter (see below)

Coat the fish with vegetable oil, and season with the salt and pepper. Grill over a very hot fire. The fish should be just barely cooked through. Place a slice of Sun-dried Tomato Butter on each steak.

Sun-dried Tomato Butter:
1/2 pound softened butter
4 tablespoons chopped sun-dried tomatoes
2 tablespoons chopped fresh basil
1/2 teaspoon crushed red chiles

Combine all the ingredients and form into a 1 1/2-inch-diameter log. Wrap the butter in plastic wrap and chill or freeze.

mango barbecued ono

Ono is a wonderful fish. It has a mild flavor and firm texture, and it goes well with ethnic or exotic preparations. If you can't find it, mahi mahi or even sea bass would make a fine substitute. There are several elements to this dish, but the extra work is well worth the effort. This is a perfect summer meal for patio dining.

Yield: 2 servings

2 (6 to 7-ounce) ono fillets
2 tablespoons vegetable oil
Pinch of salt
Pinch of pepper
4 ounces Mango Barbecue Sauce (page 177)
1/2 cup long-grain or basmati rice
6 ounces Coconut Curry Sauce (page 175)
6 tablespoons Tropical Fruit Salsa (page 178)
2 sprigs fresh cilantro, for garnish

Oil and season the fish with salt and pepper, and grill 3 to 4 minutes per side, or until just done. Baste frequently with the Mango Barbecue Sauce. Prepare the rice per package directions and, when it is done, pour in 1/2 of the Coconut Curry Sauce and toss to coat the rice. Place the rice in the center of the serving plates. Place the fish on the rice and drizzle the remaining sauce around the plate. Top the fish with the fruit salsa. Garnish with sprigs of fresh cilantro.

teriyaki
mahi mahi

*Here's a tropical fish grilled with tropical flavors.
The teriyaki gives the fish and pineapple a nicely
caramelized crust, balancing well with the orange
and pineapple notes.*

Yield: 2 portions

2 (6 to 7-ounce) mahi mahi fillets
2 thick slices of fresh pineapple
1/2 cup teriyaki glaze
2 cups assorted vegetables to stir-fry
1 1/2 cups cooked white rice
3 tablespoons freshly squeezed orange juice
1 teaspoon fresh orange peel, very finely julienned

Grill the mahi mahi and the pineapple slices, basting with 1/2 of
the teriyaki. Meanwhile, stir-fry the vegetables with the remaining
teriyaki. Pour the vegetables onto two plates and top each with a
mound of rice. Combine the juice and orange peel, and drizzle
orange peel juice on the rice. Place the fish on the rice and
garnish with pineapple slices.

This section celebrates our love of meat. After all, sometimes a great piece of meat is the only thing that will do! When those times arrive, here are some of our favorite recipes from the M&S Grill. Although our restaurants are focused primarily on fresh seafood, we're not above serving a steak or two. In several of our restaurants, we even have a concept in operation that features aged steaks and other meat and poultry dishes.

"brick-grilled" chicken breast

This dish has a very Tuscan flavor and is perfect for the heat of summer, when the local tomatoes are at their peak and their variety is plentiful. Boneless, skinless, chicken breasts will not do here. In fact, though we use skin-on breasts in our restaurants, this preparation is wonderful for split whole chickens. If bricks aren't handy, a heavy pot or cast-iron skillet works as well.

Yield: 4 servings

4 (6 to 8-ounce) skin-on chicken breasts
4 ounces Spedini Marinade (page 181)
2 cups Panzanella Salad (recipe below)
Pinch of chopped fresh parsley, for garnish

For the Panzanella Salad:
2 cups mixed varieties tomatoes, medium-diced
1/4 cup red onion, medium-diced
1/4 cup peeled and seeded cucumbers, medium-diced
2 cups medium-sized croutons
1/2 cup vinaigrette dressing

Marinate the chicken in the marinade for 6 to 8 hours, or overnight. Wrap regular house bricks with aluminum foil. Lay the chicken on the grill. Weight the chicken down with the foil-covered bricks. Grill over a hot fire until done, 12 to 15 minutes. The chicken should be nicely charred and crisp.

Prepare the salad by mixing all of the ingredients. Allow the mixture to rest while the chicken is cooking, so that the croutons absorb the dressing without getting too soggy.

Serve the Panzanella Salad as an accompaniment to the chicken. Sprinkle the parsley over both the chicken and the salad after they are placed on a plate. This preparation is excellent with crisply fried potatoes, or rice.

blackberry barbecued chicken

This is a unique barbecue sauce that takes wonderful advantage of the succulent blackberries available in the Pacific Northwest. It is sweet, smoky, and just a little spicy. The color is deep and tantalizing. The sauce works very well with the chicken here, but it also makes a terrific baste for grilled salmon. (Chef's tip: Salmon and berries are always a good combination.)

Yield: 4 servings

4 (6 to 8-ounce) skin-on chicken breasts
1 cup Blackberry Barbecue Sauce (page 173)
3 cups cheese potatoes (recipe below)
1/2 cup fresh blackberries, for garnish

Cheese Potatoes:

4 cups russet potatoes, peeled and diced	1/2 cup sliced green onion
	1/2 cup sour cream
1 1/2 cups mixed cheeses (cheddar, Jack, etc.), shredded	1 teaspoon salt
	1 teaspoon pepper

Prepare the cheese potatoes at least 1 hour before grilling the chicken. Cook the potatoes in boiling, salted water until they are fully cooked, meaning they should be a little soft, but not falling apart. Drain, then allow them to cool.

Toss the cooled potatoes with the cheese, onion, sour cream, salt, and pepper. Refrigerate for at least one hour so that the mixture becomes firm.

There are a couple of options for cooking the potatoes in the cheese-potato mixture. You can either bake them, preparing them like mashed potatoes, or, you can form them into cakes and fry them in a little oil until browned and crisp.

Grill the chicken over a hot fire, basting with the barbecue sauce, and set aside 4 tablespoons of the sauce to finish the dish.

Place the cooked potatoes and grilled chicken on serving plates with your choice of vegetable accompaniment. Spoon the remaining sauce over the chicken, garnish with the fresh blackberries, and serve.

blue cheese steak

Once in a while we serve steak with a little embellishment, which is a popular favorite with our guests. Even with the rich sauce and the blue cheese, the steak is still the number one priority. It must be of great quality, or the dish is not worth preparing. This recipe is a treat and a way to do a little more than simply grilling a steak.

Yield: 2 servings

1 (1 1/2-inch-thick) strip steak
2 teaspoons Montreal seasoning
1/2 cup red wine
2 tablespoons brandy
1/2 cup prepared demi-glace sauce
1/4 cup crumbled blue cheese
2 tablespoons sliced green onion (green part only)

Season the steak with the Montreal seasoning and grill to your desired doneness. Heat the wine in a sauce pan and reduce while the steak is cooking. Remove the sauce pan from the heat and pour in the brandy. Carefully return the pan to medium-high heat. The brandy may flame. Allow the flame to die down, and then add the demi-glace. Continue to reduce over medium-high heat for another 2 to 3 minutes.

Remove the cooked steak to a plate and allow it to rest for 1 to 2 minutes. Slice the steak, across the grain, into serving pieces. Place the steak pieces on the serving plates and pour the sauce over them. Scatter the blue cheese over the steaks and serve with your favorite potato or vegetable.

chipotle-brined pork loin

Brining is an old-fashioned technique that has returned to favor over the last few years. Pork is the ideal meat for taking advantage of the benefits of brining. Pork is firm, but very tender, it cooks quickly, develops a great color, and it retains moisture. This recipe is full of great flavors, showing why brining has become so popular with chefs throughout the country.

Yield: 4 servings

2 1/2 pounds center-cut boneless pork loin roast
1 quart prepared chipotle brine (recipe below)
2 tablespoons Southwest seasoning
1 cup Southwest Barbecue Sauce (page 180)
1/4 cup prepared Peach Chutney (page 178)

For the brine:
1 quart water
1/4 cup kosher salt
1/4 cup sugar
2 tablespoons chipotle pepper purée
1 teaspoon allspice

Prepare the brine by mixing all the ingredients together and allowing the sugar and salt to dissolve. Submerge the pork loin completely in the brine and soak ovenight.

Rinse the brined pork loin under cold water and wipe it dry. Slice the loin into 8 equal pieces. Dust the meat with the Southwest seasoning, and grill over a hot fire for 4 to 5 minutes per side. *The pork should be cooked through, but will be a little pink from the brining.* Baste liberally with the barbecue sauce during grilling, especially toward the end of the cooking time. Place the grilled pork on serving plates with your favorite accompaniments and top the meat with the chutney.

marinated steaks

To us, there are two ways to grill steaks: straight on the grill with either a small amount of seasoning, or marinated before cooking. Which flavoring method we use is determined by the cut of the meat. Strip steaks, filet mignon, top sirloin, and rib-eyes get the simple treatment. They are consistently tender and moist, so the simpler the treatment the better. There are other great steaks available to grill, and we use them as well. Marinating adds tenderness and juiciness to an otherwise tough-as-nails cut of meat. Don't avoid these cuts, because after they've been marinated some are the most flavorful cuts of all.

We like to serve this type of steak with grilled onions and maybe a condiment sauce like fresh salsa or a garlic mayonnaise.

Yield: 4 servings

4 portions steak (flank, skirt, or flat-iron)
1/2 cup Spedini Marinade (page 181)
1/2 cup barbecue sauce (your favorite brand)

Marinate the steaks in equal parts of the Spedini marinade and barbecue sauce for 3 to 4 hours. Grill the steaks over a very hot fire to your desired doneness. (These types of steaks, though well marinated, should be served medium-rare to rare, as they tend to dry out very quickly when cooked beyond these stages.)

world-class
pot pie

If you aren't making world-class *pot pie, why bother?*
We think this recipe defines world-class, and so do our guests.
Almost everyone has a great pot pie recipe from their mom
or grandma, so we're really not trying to say ours is the best.
(But it is world-class.) Try it and decide for yourself.
We make individual pot-pie casseroles in our restaurants.
You can do the same or bake them in a larger baking dish
for a "scoop and go" meal for the entire family.

Yield: 6 servings

1 prepared pie dough (page 179)
1 1/2 pounds boneless, skinless
   chicken breasts
3 tablespoons vegetable oil
2 cups chicken stock (canned or
   homemade)
5 tablespoons butter
3/4 cup diced onion
3/4 cup diced celery

3/4 cup diced carrot
1/2 cup plus 2 tablespoons flour
1 1/2 cup heavy cream
Large pinch of salt
Large pinch of pepper
1/2 teaspoon dried thyme
1/4 cup sherry
1/2 cup frozen peas, thawed

Preheat the oven to 400°F. Roll out the pie dough for a large, single-crust pie, or for six individual pies. Dice the chicken into 1-inch pieces and sauté in oil to brown lightly. Add the stock and simmer for a couple of minutes. Remove the chicken meat with a slotted spoon and set the stock aside. Return the pan to the heat, add the butter, and sauté the vegetables until they just start to soften, 2 to 3 minutes. Add the flour to the pan to form a roux, and cook, stirring constantly, for 4 to 5 minutes. Add the cream, the reserved stock, and the seasonings, and simmer until thickened. Add the sherry, peas, and the reserved chicken, and simmer for 2 to 3 minutes. Pour the mixture into the baking dish or divide it equally into 6 individual oven casseroles. Lay the pie crust over the top of the casseroles and seal the edges as you would for any other pie. Bake for 20 minutes, or until the crust is golden brown.

grilled chicken WITH michigan cherry barbecue sauce

This delicious barbecue sauce comes from our Midwest region, where the cherries are a special treat. Dried cherries are sweet, tart, and deeply flavored. Here we make a fabulous sauce that complements grilled chicken and creates a wonderful interaction with blue cheese. It has been a favorite in many of our restaurants for years.

Yield: 4 servings

4 boneless, skinless chicken breasts
1/4 cup vegetable oil
1 teaspoon Kosher salt
1 teaspoon paprika
1 teaspoon freshly ground black pepper
1 1/2 cup Michigan Cherry Barbecue Sauce (page 177)
1/2 cup crumbled Gorgonzola cheese

Coat the chicken breasts with the oil, and season with the salt, pepper, and paprika. Grill the chicken over a hot fire, basting with small amounts of the sauce. Place the grilled chicken onto serving plates, and top with 1 to 2 tablespoons of the barbecue sauce. Scatter the cheese over the chicken and serve with your favorite rice and vegetables.

meatloaf

Just like pot pie, everyone has an opinion and a favorite recipe for meatloaf. Whether your mom made it, or you've developed your own recipe over the years, there's a family-favorite meatloaf in most everyone's recipe files. And, as old-fashioned as it is, the smell of meatloaf in the oven can bring back distant memories for some, intense emotions for many. We humbly offer our version, which has been a staple of our lunch menus for the past twenty years.

Yield: 6 servings

1/2 pound fresh mushrooms
1/2 cup diced onion
2 pounds ground beef
1 pound ground pork
1/4 cup Heinz Chili Sauce
1 egg
1 tablespoon chopped garlic
1 tablespoon Worcestershire sauce
3/4 cup Panko bread crumbs
1 tablespoon salt
1 tablespoon pepper
1 tablespoon garlic powder

Preheat the oven to 350°F. Grind the onions and mushrooms very finely in a food processor. Combine all the ingredients, and blend, but do not over-mix. The meatloaf may be baked free-form on a baking sheet or pressed into a loaf pan. Bake until internal temperature reaches 160°F on a meat or quick-read thermometer. Allow the meatloaf to rest for 10 to 15 minutes before slicing. Serve with your favorite brown gravy.

desserts

For so many of us, a meal just isn't complete without dessert. Our dessert trays are always filled with great, traditional, Americana-style selections to entice our guests into finishing their McCormick & Schmick's dining experience on the highest of notes. We offer our favorites here to add to your collection and satisfy every sweet tooth in your family.

triple-chocolate, ice-cream sandwich

This is more of a construction project than a recipe, but if you choose to buy all of the components, this is perhaps the fastest and easiest "recipe to WOW 'em" around. On the other hand, if you are so inclined, you can bake your own cookies, make your own ice cream and chocolate sauce, and really impress everyone. Whatever you choose, this dessert evokes great childhood memories in a very grown-up style.

Yield: 1 serving

2 (4-inch) dark chocolate chip cookies
1 scoop chocolate ice cream
3 tablespoons of chocolate sauce
Confectioners' sugar, to dust

Place one cookie on a serving plate and top it with a scoop of ice cream. Place the other cookie on top and you have what looks like a softball between two Frisbees. Drizzle chocolate sauce over everything and dust the plate with the confectioners' sugar.

That's it...just wait till you dig in!

chocolate hazelnut pie

This is the Pacific Northwest's answer to Southern-style pecan pie. A flaky crust, a gooey center, and a layer of toasted hazelnuts and chocolate chips. It's been a standard on the dessert tray at the Harborside Restaurant in Portland, Oregon since we opened. Toss out the diet and pass the whipped cream.

Yield: 1 (9-inch) pie

1 prepared pie dough (page 179)
1 cup sugar
1 1/3 cups dark corn syrup
7 tablespoons butter, cubed
6 eggs
1/2 tablespoon vanilla
1 1/2 cups hazelnuts, toasted, peeled and very coarsely chopped or halved
2/3 cup semi-sweet chocolate chips

Preheat the oven to 300°F.

Prepare and roll out the pie crust and fit into a 9-inch pie pan. Chill or freeze the shell until ready to fill.

Combine the sugar and syrup in a saucepan and bring to a boil, stirring constantly over medium heat. Cook at a boil for 2 minutes. Remove and cool for 10 to 15 minutes.

Melt 1 1/2 tablespoons of the butter in another saucepan and allow to brown slightly. Remove and cool.

Beat the eggs. When the sugar mixture has cooled, add it to the eggs slowly, stirring constantly. Add the brown butter, the remaining cubed butter, and the vanilla, and stir until butter has melted and the mixture is well blended.

Spread nuts and chocolate chips evenly over the bottom of the pie crust and pour in the egg-sugar-butter mixture.

Bake for 1 hour and 15 minutes, until the filling has puffed up 1 to 1 1/2 inches and is firm to the touch. Allow to cool thoroughly before cutting. (The filling will settle during cooling.)

Approximate preparation time: 2 hours

marionberry pie

Simple, but absolutely delicious, this is a great example of the old-fashioned "American" desserts that are the foundation of our dessert programs. The key is great-tasting berries— whether they are fresh or frozen, make sure that they are big and juicy.

Marionberries, indigenous to Oregon, are best for this pie, as they are large, full of fruit flavor, and very juicy. Loganberries or other berries are just as tasty.

Yield: 1 (9-inch) pie

1 prepared pie dough (page 179)
3 cups marionberries, fresh or frozen
1/2 cup sugar
1 1/2 tablespoons flour
1/4 teaspoon salt
2 tablespoons butter

Preheat the oven to 350°F.

Roll the dough out for 2 (9-inch) crusts. Place one of the sheets of dough into the pie pan and tuck the edges in place. Toss the remaining ingredients together to blend. Taste a berry and, if it isn't sweet enough, add a bit more sugar. Mound the berry mixture into the pie pan and cover with the remaining sheet of dough. Crimp and trim the edges and cut slits in the top. Bake for 1 hour at 350°F, or until the crust is golden brown. Allow the pie to cool for at least 1 hour before slicing. Serve with vanilla ice cream.

three-berry cobbler

This is one of the most popular desserts, an old-fashioned favorite that will please the most jaded of palates. Naturally, it's best when berries are fresh, but we serve it year-round using frozen berries from the summer harvest. Try topping this with vanilla ice cream for the best treat this side of heaven.

Yield: 4 (2/3 cup) custard dishes

Crust:

1 1/4 cups flour
1 1/2 teaspoons baking powder
1 tablespoon of sugar
1/4 teaspoon salt

1 stick butter, cut into cubes and
  kept cold
1 egg
1/3 cup milk

Filling:

5 cups mixed berries
2 tablespoons water
1 1/2 tablespoons cornstarch

1 tablespoon freshly squeezed
  lemon juice
3/4 cup sugar

Preheat the oven to 350°F.

Crumble together the flour, baking powder, sugar, and butter until it is the texture of coarse cornmeal. Blend in the egg and milk. Mix and form into a ball. Roll out the dough on a floured surface to 1/8-inch thickness. Using a template that is the same size and shape as the dish or dishes you are going to bake the cobbler in (these can be 2/3 cup individual dishes or a larger Pyrex baking dish), cut the dough and chill it while you prepare the berries. Combine all ingredients for the filling in a saucepan and bring to a boil, stirring frequently. When the mixture is thick and syrupy, remove from heat. Spoon the mixture into baking dishes. Cover loosely with the crust, place baking dishes on baking sheet a and bake for 15 minutes, until the crust is lightly browned and the berry filling is bubbling out around the edges. Let cool before serving.

Approximate preparation time: 1 hour

deep-dish apple pie

We just had to revive this beauty, which dates back to the early days of the original McCormick & Schmick's Seafood Restaurant in Portland, Oregon. You need a 9-inch deep-dish pie pan with a removable bottom to do it justice.

Yield: 1 (9 by 4-inch) pie

Crust:
2 cups flour
4 tablespoons sugar
1/2 teaspoon salt
10 tablespoons butter, cold and cut into small cubes
3 to 4 tablespoons water
1 egg yolk

Filling:
16 cups sliced apples (14 to 16 large Granny Smiths or Newtons)
1 tablespoon freshly squeezed lemon juice
1 tablespoon cinnamon
6 tablespoons flour
1 1/3 cups sugar
1/4 cup water

Streusel Topping:
1 cup flour
1 cup dark brown sugar
6 tablespoons butter or margarine

Remove all but the lower rack of your oven and preheat to 300°F.

Prepare the crust by combining the flour, sugar, and salt and working in the butter until the mixture resembles coarse cornmeal. Add the water and egg yolk and combine just enough to form a roll. Wrap in plastic and refrigerate for at least 1 hour.

The filling is prepared by combining the sliced apples with the remaining ingredients and blending thoroughly. Make sure all the apples are well coated. Roll the pie dough out to about 18 inches in diameter for the deep-dish tin. Line the tin with the dough, and flute the edge. Add the apple mixture so that it mounds well above the top of the shell at least 2 inches or 3 inches in the center.

Combine the streusel ingredients and sprinkle liberally over the entire surface of the apples, so that there is a good coating of streusel. Bake at 300°F for 2 1/2 hours, until well browned. Remove the pie, allow to cool for 1 to 2 hours, then carefully and gently press the apples down into the pie until they are just about level with the crust. Refrigerate overnight to allow the pie to set. This procedure will firm the texture of the filling. Remove the pie from the tin. (This is the reason you need a removable bottom—trying to cut this pie out of a tin does not work.) When you are ready to serve, reheat the pie and serve with a scoop of vanilla ice cream.

Approximate preparation time: 1 hour preparation; 3 hours baking; 2 hours cooling; overnight to chill.

basics

asian cucumber salad

Yield: 3 cups

1 1/2 cups cucumbers, peeled and seeded
1/4 cup carrots, thinly julienned
1/4 cup red onion, thinly julienned
1/2 cup wakame salad, prepared
1/4 cup rice wine vinegar
1 tablespoon sugar
3/4 teaspoon salt
3/4 teaspoon Thai chili paste
1 tablespoon sesame oil

Make 1 hour, but not more than 3 to 4 hours, before using. Slice the cucumbers thinly and toss them with the carrots, onion, and wakame. Mix the remaining ingredients in a separate bowl to dissolve the sugar and pour the blend over the cucumber mixture. Toss well.

avocado salsa

Yield: 1 cup

1 large avocado, diced to about 1/2 inch
1 1/2 tablespoons finely diced onion
1 teaspoon minced jalapeño pepper
1 1/2 teaspoons chopped fresh cilantro
1 tablespoon freshly squeezed lime juice
2 tablespoons purchased salsa
Pinch of salt
Combine all the ingredients and fold to blend. Be careful not to smash the avocados.

blackberry barbecue sauce

Yield: 1 cup

1 tablespoon Major Grey's Chutney
1/2 tablespoon sugar
1 tablespoon rice wine vinegar
1/2 tablespoon freshly squeezed lemon juice
1/2 tablespoon sambal oelek
1/4 cup minced red onion
1/2 pound frozen blackberries
2 tablespoons purchased barbecue sauce

Purée all the ingredients except the berries in a food processor. Purée the berries separately and pass them through a sieve. Combine all the ingredients and blend thoroughly.

buerre blanc sauce

Yield: 1 cup

6 ounces white wine
3 ounces white wine vinegar
3 whole black peppercorns
1 shallot, quartered
1 cup heavy cream
6 ounces cold, unsalted butter, cut into pieces
3 ounces cold butter, cut into pieces

Combine wine, vinegar, peppercorns, and shallot in a noncorrosive saucepan (stainless steel, Teflon, claphalon). Reduce until the mixture is just 1 to 2 tablespoons and has the consistency of syrup. Add the cream and reduce again until the mixture is 3 to 4 tablespoons and very syrupy. Remove the pan from heat. Add the butter pieces, about 2 ounces at a time, stirring constantly and allowing each piece to melt in before adding more. (If the mixture cools too much, the butter will not melt completely and you will have to reheat it slightly.) Strain and hold warm on a stove-top trivet or in a double-boiler over very low heat until you are ready to use.

Note: To make Lemon Butter Sauce, replace the white wine vinegar with 2 tablespoons of freshly squeezed lemon juice.

buttered bread crumbs

1/4 cup butter, melted
1/2 cup Panko breadcrumbs
1/2 cup Progresso Italian Breadcrumbs
2 tablespoons chopped fresh parsley

Place all ingredients in a bowl. Blend well.

cashew dipping sauce

Yield: about 1 1/2 cups
1 cup sweet Thai chili sauce
1/4 cup minced fresh cilantro
1/2 tablespoon freshly squeezed lemon
  juice
1 tablespoon rice wine vinegar
2 ounces unsalted cashews

Preheat oven to 350°F. Combine all ingredients except cashews. Roast cashews on a baking sheet for 10 minutes until

brown. Chop the cashews in a food processor until they are coarsely chopped. Combine the cashews with the mixture and blend thoroughly.

cheese sauce

Yield: about 2 cups
4 ounces butter
1/2 cup diced yellow onions
4 ounces flour
1 cup heavy cream
1 cup whole milk
Pinch of salt
Pinch of freshly ground black pepper
Pinch of nutmeg
Pinch of dry mustard
1/2 pound shredded sharp cheddar cheese

Sauté the onions in the butter until soft. Add the flour slowly while stirring to make the roux. Cook for 3 to 4 minutes over medium heat. While stirring constantly, add the cream and the milk. Add the seasonings and the cheese, and simmer over low heat until thickened and smooth. If a more refined sauce is desired, you may strain the sauce.

chipotle aïoli

Yield: 1 cup
2 tablespoons sweet Thai chili sauce
1 tablespoon chipotle purée
1/2 tablespoon freshly squeezed lime
  juice
1/2 tablespoon chopped fresh cilantro
1 cup mayonnaise

Combine the ingredients and purée in a food processor.

cilantro jalapeño crème

Yield: 1 cup

1 cup sour cream
2 teaspoons fresh cilantro
1 tablespoon jalapeño pepper
Pinch of salt
Pinch of white pepper
2 teaspoons freshly squeezed lemon juice

Combine all ingredients in a food processor. Mix on high to blend well.

cilantro-orange dressing

Yield: 1 cup

1/2 cup mayonnaise
3 tablespoons orange juice concentrate
1 tablespoon honey
1 tablespoon rice wine vinegar
1/2 tablespoon sambal oelek
1/2 teaspoon powdered ginger
2 tablespoons chopped fresh cilantro
1/2 teaspoon vanilla extract

Combine all ingredients and blend thoroughly.

citrus marinade

Yield: 1 cup

4 oranges, squeezed
2 limes, squeezed
1 lemon, squeezed
2 tablespoons finely chopped fresh cilantro
2 tablespoons minced ginger
1 tablespoon minced garlic

Combine all ingredients and blend well.

clarified butter

Any amount of butter

Heat desired amount of butter in a sauce pan until fully melted and beginning to boil. Turn heat off and allow the butter to rest for about 10 minutes, or until the milk solids and the oil have separated. Skim the milk solids off the top surface of the butter. Save them to flavor vegetables or other items, as they are full of flavor. Slowly and carefully begin to pour off the clear "oil" until you begin to have trouble separating the oil from the remaining milk solids in the bottom of the pan. Save the remaining milk solids for other uses.

cocktail sauce

Yield: about 2 cups

1 cup purchased chili sauce
1/2 cup ketchup
2 tablespoons horseradish
1 teaspoon freshly squeezed lemon juice
1 teaspoon Worcestershire
1/2 teaspoon dry mustard
1/2 teaspoon freshly ground black pepper
1 teaspoon Tabasco sauce
1/4 teaspoon salt

Combine all ingredients and mix well.

coconut curry sauce

Yield: 2 cups

1 cup coconut milk
1 tablespoon freshly squeezed lime juice
1/4 cup peanut butter
1 cup chicken stock
3 tablespoons yellow Thai curry paste
2 tablespoons chopped fresh cilantro
2 teaspoons kosher salt

Combine all ingredients in a small sauce pan and simmer for 8 to 10 minutes over medium-high heat, until the sauce is somewhat thickened.

corn bisque

Yield: 2 cups
2 cobs yellow corn (kernels removed and cobs set aside)
3 cups chicken stock
1 teaspoon diced shallots
1 teaspoon minced garlic
1/4 pound butter
3 tablespoons flour
1 tablespoon sugar
1 cup heavy cream
1/4 teaspoon tumeric
Salt and pepper

Combine the corn cobs and the chicken stock in a small sauce pot to form a corn stock. Bring to a boil and allow to cook for about 30 minutes on medium heat. Strain the stock and set it aside. Sauté the shallots and garlic in the butter until translucent. Add the flour to make a roux. Add the sugar, corn stock, and corn kernels. Bring the mixture to a boil and decrease to a simmer. Add the seasonings and cook for 15 minutes. Add the cream and increase temperature and let mixture boil for 5 minutes. Remove the mixture from the heat and strain.

creole sauce

Yield: 6 servings
6 ounces diced celery (large dice)
6 ounces diced onion (large dice)
6 ounces diced green bell pepper (large dice)
2 ounces puréed roasted garlic

3 ounces butter
12 ounces diced canned tomatoes
4 ounces tomato sauce
1/2 ounce beef base
1 tablespoon dried oregano
2 teaspoons cayenne pepper
2 teaspoons McCormick Cajun Spice
1/2 teaspoon paprika
1/8 teaspoon freshly ground black pepper
2 teaspoons dried basil

Sauté the vegetables and garlic in butter until soft. Combine the remaining ingredients and simmer for 20 minutes.

dill cream sauce

Yield: about 2 cups
2 ounces butter
2 ounces diced yellow onions
2 ounces flour
2 cups chicken stock
3/4 cup sour cream
Pinch of kosher salt
Pinch of freshly ground pepper
2 tablespoons chopped fresh dill

Sauté the onions lightly in the butter. Add the flour slowly while stirring to make a roux. Cook for an additional 3 to 4 minutes over low heat. Add the chicken stock and simmer until thick and smooth. Strain the sauce. Add the remaining ingredients, stirring well to blend the sour cream into the sauce. Do not let the sauce boil after adding the sour cream.

gazpacho

Yield: 2 quarts
4 pounds canned, peeled tomatoes in juice
1/2 pound peeled and seeded cucumbers

1/4 pound seeded and chopped green peppers
4 tablespoons chopped green onion
2 garlic cloves
6 ounces tomato juice
1 tablespoon sherry vinegar
1 tablespoon red wine vinegar
1/2 cup Extra Virgin olive oil
1/2 tablespoon kosher salt
1 teaspoon freshly ground black pepper
1 teaspoon Tabasco
1 teaspoon cumin

Drain the tomatoes and save 1 1/2 cups of the juice. Combine the tomatoes, cucumbers, green peppers, green onions, and garlic. Purée the mixture, in small batches, using a food processor. Combine all the remaining ingredients and blend thoroughly. Chill the soup overnight.

jamaican rum butter sauce

Yield: about 1 1/2 cups
1/2 vanilla bean
1/4 cup white rum
1/4 cup dark rum
Pinch of saffron
1 tablespoon freshly squeezed lime juice
1/4 minced habanero pepper
1 tablespoon sugar
1/2 pound cold butter, cut into 1-inch pieces

Split the vanilla bean in half and place into a sauce pan. Add both types of rum, the saffron, lime juice, pepper, and sugar. Reduce the mixture to 4 tablespoons over medium heat. Remove the pan from the heat and stir in the butter, to form into a sauce—a little butter at a time, allowing each piece to melt before adding more.

mango barbecue sauce

Yield: 1 cup
4 tablespoons coconut milk
1/2 cup chutney (use your favorite brand)
1 mango, peeled and diced
2 tablespoons chopped fresh cilantro
4 tablespoons purchased barbecue sauce

Combine all ingredients in a food processor and purée.

michigan cherry barbecue sauce

Yield: 1 1/2 cups
1 cup dried cherries
1 cup hot water
1 cup ketchup
1 tablespoon butter
1/2 cup small diced yellow onion
1/3 cup packed brown sugar
1 tablespoon yellow mustard
1 tablespoon Tabasco
2 teaspoons kosher salt

Plump the cherries in the hot water for 10 minutes. Lightly sauté the onions in butter until soft. Add the remaining ingredients and cook on low flame for 5 minutes. Drain the cherries and add them to the sauce. Cook for an additional 5 minutes. Blend the mixture in a food processor until it has a semi-smooth appearance.

newburg sauce

Yield: 1 quart
5 tablespoons butter
2 tablespoons minced onion
1/2 tablespoon paprika

2 ounces flour
3 cups hot milk
1 cup heavy cream
Pinch of salt
Pinch of white pepper
Dash of Tabasco
2 tablespoons lobster base
1/4 cup dry sherry

Melt the butter in a sauce pot. Add the onions and sauté until transparent. Add the paprika. Add the flour to make roux. Cook for 8 to 10 minutes, but do not brown. Add the hot milk and blend well. Add the cream and blend well. Add the remaining seasonings and simmer for 15 minutes, stirring often. Strain and stir in the sherry.

northwest berry sauce

Yield: 2 cups
1 1/2 cups frozen, mixed berries
1/4 cup water
1/4 cup white wine
1/4 cup white wine vinegar
1 large chopped shallot (or 2 tablespoons chopped onion)
4 to 5 whole black peppercorns
1/4 cup heavy cream
1/4 pound very cold butter, cut into 1/2-inch cubes

Place the berries in a sauce pan with 1/4 cup water and simmer on low heat until the berries are mushy and the mixture is slightly thickened, about 10 minutes.

While the berries are cooking, place the white wine, the vinegar, the shallots, peppercorns, and heavy cream into another sauce pan. Reduce the mixture over medium-high heat, stirring occasionally, until it reaches the consistency of corn

syrup. Strain out the shallot and peppercorns. Strain the berry mixture into the wine mixture and discard the berry solids. Remove the mixture from heat and whisk, adding the butter 2 to 3 cubes at a time.

tropical fruit salsa

Yield: about 1 cup
2 tablespoons fresh mango, diced to about 1/4 inch
2 tablespoons fresh papaya, diced to about 1/4 inch
4 tablespoons fresh pineapple, diced to about 1/4 inch
2 tablespoons finely diced red onion
1 tablespoon finely diced green bell pepper
1 tablespoon finely diced red bell pepper
2 teaspoons freshly squeezed lime juice
Pinch of salt
Pinch of freshly ground white pepper
Pinch of cumin
1 teaspoon chopped fresh cilantro
2 splashes triple sec (optional)

Combine all ingredients. Season to taste. Toss to blend.

peach chutney

Yield: about 1 1/2 cups
1/2 cup Major Grey's Chutney
1 cup peeled, diced peaches, fresh or frozen
2 teaspoons freshly squeezed lime juice
1/2 teaspoon crushed red chiles

Purée all ingredients in a blender or food processor on "pulse" until the mixture is coarsely chopped.

pesto bacon crust

Yield: 1 pound
1/2 pound bacon
8 ounces basil
1 ounce pine nuts
20 cloves garlic
4 tablespoons Extra virgin olive oil

Grind bacon in a food processor to make a fine paste. Remove the paste and refrigerate. In the same food processor, process the basil, garlic, and olive oil to make pesto. Mix the pesto and bacon paste together.

pie and tart dough

Yield: 1 (9-inch) crust
1 cup flour
Pinch of salt
6 tablespoons very cold butter, cut into
   1/2-inch cubes
2 tablespoons beaten whole egg
1 tablespoon very cold water

Blend the flour, salt, and butter until the mixture resembles cornmeal. Add the egg and water and form the dough into a ball. Do not overwork the dough.

raspberry-balsamic glaze

Yield: about 2 cups
1 cup raspberry jam
1 teaspoon freshly squeezed lemon juice
2 tablepsoons sugar
1 cup balsamic vinegar

Place all ingredients in a small sauce pan. Bring to a boil and allow the sauce to reduce by 1/4 of the original amount, about 1/2 cup. Mix, using a small handheld mixer or very carefully, in a blender. Strain well to remove all seeds from the sauce. Serve at room temperature.

red onion relish

Yield: 1 cup
1 finely diced medium red onion
2 finely diced garlic cloves
3 tablespoons chopped fresh cilantro
1 teaspoon sambal oelek
1 tablespoon red wine vinegar
3/4 cup red wine
1 1/2 tablespoons olive oil
1 ounce capers
Salt and black pepper

Gently sauté the onion and garlic until tender. Remove from heat and set aside. In a separate pot, reduce red wine to 1/4 of a cup. Combine all the ingredients and toss well. Salt and pepper to taste.

roasted corn salsa

Yield: 1 1/2 cup
1 tablespoon oil
3/4 cup thawed frozen corn
2 tablespoons red bell pepper, diced to
   1/4 inch
2 tablespoons green bell pepper, diced
   to 1/4 inch
2 tablespoons red onion, diced to 1/4 inch
2 teaspoons chopped fresh cilantro
1 teaspoon cumin
Pinch of salt
Pinch of pepper
1 teaspoon freshly squeezed lime juice
2 tablespoons purchased salsa

Char the corn in the oil in a very hot sauté pan. Combine the remaining ingredients and blend.

roasted tomato sauce

Yield: 3 cups
5 pounds Roma tomatoes
1/4 cup vegetable oil
1 cup diced yellow onions
1/2 cup diced celery
1/2 cup diced carrots
5 garlic cloves, minced
6 tablespoons olive oil
4 tablespoons butter
1/2 cup tomato paste
4 tablespoons chopped fresh basil
1 tablespoon dried oregano
1 tablespoon kosher salt
2 tablespoons freshly ground black
  pepper
1/2 tablespoon crushed red chili
  flakes

Preheat oven to 250°F. Slice each tomato into 4 to 5 slices. Arrange the tomatoes in a single layer on a foil-lined sheet pan or cookie sheet. Sprinkle the tomatoes with the vegetable oil and bake for 2 hours or until slightly shriveled. Remove the tomatoes, chop them roughly and set aside. Sauté the onions, celery, and carrots in the olive oil and butter over medium-high heat until soft. Add the garlic and continue to cook for 3 to 4 minutes. Add the roasted tomatoes and the remaining ingredients. Simmer the sauce for 15 to 20 minutes over low heat.

southwest barbecue sauce

Yield: 1 quart
2 tablespoons vegetable oil
3/4 cup chopped yellow onions
2 tablespoons minced garlic
1 tablespoon minced jalapeño peppers
2 tablespoons Worchestershire sauce
1/2 cup tomato paste
1/2 cup cider vinegar
1/4 cup brown sugar
1 tablespoon cumin
1 tablespoon chili powder
1/4 cup chopped chipotle peppers
2 cups chicken stock

Sauté the onions and garlic in the oil until slightly browned. Add the remaining ingredients and simmer for 20 to 30 minutes, or until somewhat thickened.

southwestern corn crust batter

Yield: enough for 6 servings of fish fillets
1/2 cup flour
1/4 cup yellow cornmeal
3/4 tablespoon baking powder
1/2 tablespoon kosher salt
1 1/2 cups milk
1 egg
2 tablespoons melted butter
1/4 tablespoon Tabasco
2 cups fresh corn
1/2 cup chopped green onion
1/8 cup finely diced poblano chiles
1 diced jalapeño pepper

Combine the flour, cornmeal, baking powder, and kosher salt in a mixing bowl. Mix the milk, egg, butter, and

Tabasco in a separate bowl. Combine the 2 mixtures and blend well. Add the corn, onions, and pepper, and chiles and fold together. Cover and refrigerate until ready to use.

spedini marinade

Yield: 2 cups
6 tablespoons white balsamic vinegar
2 tablespoons granulated garlic
1 teaspoon paprika
1 teaspoon Tabasco
1/2 tablespoon salt
1/2 tablespoon freshly ground black
  pepper
1 teaspoon chili powder
1 tablespoon oregano
1 1/2 cups olive oil

Combine all ingredients and blend well. Stir well prior to use.

tamarind glace

Yield: 1 cup
1/2 pound fresh tamarind pods
1 cup water
1/4 cup honey
1 small hot chili (jalapeño, arbol,
  serrano, etc.)
2 tablespoons oil
1 tablespoon cornstarch, mixed with
  1 tablespoon of water
3 green onions, julienned

Place the tamarind pods in a bowl, cover them with warm water, and let stand for about 30 minutes. Peel the pods and squeeze the pulp out with your fingers. Place the tamarind pulp in

a sauce pan and boil for about 15 minutes. Pass the pulp through a strainer to remove seeds and veins. Toast the chili in the oil until browned. Mince the chili and add it and the honey to the sauce. Add the cornstarch to thicken to a medium consistency. Allow the sauce to cool. Add the julienned green onions when the sauce is cold throughout.

tartar sauce

Yield: 3 cups
1/3 cup finely minced celery
1/3 cup finely minced onion
2 cups mayonnaise, homemade or
  purchased
2 tablespoons freshly squeezed lemon
  juice
1 teaspoon Worcestershire sauce
Pinch of salt
Pinch of dry mustard
Pinch of pepper
2 tablespoons dill pickle relish

Combine all ingredients and mix well.

thousand island dressing

Yield: 4 cups
1/2 cup finely diced celery
1/2 cup finely diced onion
2 cups mayonnaise, homemade or purchased
1 tablespoon Worcestershire sauce
1 tablespoon prepared horseradish
3/4 cup chili sauce
2 tablespoons freshly squeezed lemon
  juice

2 tablespoons dill pickle relish
Pinch of salt
Pinch of pepper

Combine all ingredients and mix well.

wasabi aïoli

Yield: 1 cup
2 teaspoons wasabi powder
1 teaspoon orange juice
1 teaspoon freshly squeezed lime juice
2 teaspoons pickled ginger
1 egg yolk
1 cup mayonnaise

Combine the wasabi powder, orange juice, lime juice, pickled ginger, and mayonnaise in a food processor and purée. Allow the mixture to rest for 10 minutes and then purée again, adding the egg yolk. Blend the mixture to a mayonnaise-like consistency.

concordance

ahi, see tuna

appetizers

barbecue

butters

catfish

char

chicken

chowder

clams

cod

corvina

crab

seafood

Broiled Seafood Platter, 75
Seafood & Corn Chowder, 35
Seafood Chili, 127
Seafood Cocktails, 8
Seafood Fettuccini Alfredo, 49
Seafood Macaroni & Cheese, 67
Seafood Newburg, 73
Shellfish Pan Roast, 71
Spenger's Fish Tacos, 45

shrimp

Crab, Shrimp, & Artichoke Dip, 16
Dungeness Crab & Bay Shrimp Cakes, 4
Dungeness Crab & Shrimp Melt, 44
Fettuccini Alfredo with Boursin &
   Grilled Shrimp, 55
Gazpacho Shrimp Cocktail, 19
Grilled Prawns with Tamarind Glace, 138
Grilled Shrimp & Fruit Salad, 27
Grilled Shrimp with Blackberry
   Barbecue Sauce, 141
Halibut & Salmon Medallions with
   Potato-Shrimp Cake, 88
Lobster & Bay Shrimp Crepes, 101
Lobster & Shrimp Enchilada, 119
Panchetta-Wrapped Prawns, 17
Scampi-Style Shrimp & Roasted Tomato
   Linguini, 59
Southwest Bay Shrimp & Avocado
   Salad, 29
Southwest-Bronzed Halibut & Prawns, 96
Spicy Shrimp Linguini, 53
Stuffed Salmon with Crab & Shrimp, 91

snapper

Corn-Crusted Snapper, 100

swordfish

Grilled Swordfish, 143
Swordfish Piccata, 76

tilapia

Cashew-Crusted Tilapia, 115

trout

Grilled Rainbow Trout, 139

tuna

Grilled Tuna with Mandarin Oranges &
   Avocado Salsa, 129
Seared Rare Ahi, 11
Tuna Au Poivre with Port Demi Glace, 107
Tuna Takashimi, 111
Yellowfin Tuna Burger, 40